Aristide Fumagalli

JOURNEYING IN LOVE

Pope Francis' Moral Theology

LIBERIA EDITRICE VATICANA

Published in Australia by

© Copyright 2019 Coventry Press

Coventry Press
33 Scoresby Road
Bayswater Vic. 3153
Australia

Translated into English by Salesians of Don Bosco of the Province of Mary Help of Christians of Australia and the Pacific

ISBN 9780987643148

© Copyright 2017 - Libreria Editrice Vaticana
00120 Città del Vaticano
Tel. 06.698.81032 - Fax 06.698.84716
commerciale.lev@spc.va

All rights reserved. Other than for the purposes and subject to the conditions prescribed under the *Copyright Act*, no part of this publication may be reproduced, stored in a retrieval system, or transmitted in any form or by any means, electronic, mechanical, photocopying, recording or otherwise, without the prior permission of the publisher.

Cataloguing-in-Publication entry is available from the National Library of Australia http:/catalogue.nla.gov.au/.

Printed in Australia

www.coventrypress.com.au

SERIES
THE THEOLOGY OF POPE FRANCIS

JURGEN WERBICK: *God's weakness for humankind.* Pope Francis' view of God

LUCIO CASULA: *Faces, gestures and places.* Pope Francis' Christology

PETER HÜNERMANN: *Human beings according to Christ today.* Pope Francis' Anthropology

ROBERTO REPOLE: *The dream of a gospel-inspired Church.* Pope Francis' Ecclesiology

CARLOS GALLI: *Christ, Mary, the Church and the peoples.* Pope Francis' Mariology

SANTIAGO MADRIGAL TERRAZAS: *'Unity Prevails over Conflict'.* Pope Francis' Ecumenism

ARISTIDE FUMAGALLI: *Journeying in love.* Pope Francis' Moral Theology

JUAN CARLOS SCANNONE: *The Gospel of Mercy in the spirit of discernment.* Pope Francis' Social Ethics

MARINELLA PERRONI: *Kerygma and prophecy.* Pope Francis' Biblical Hermeneutics

PIERO CODA: *'The Church is the Gospel'.* At the sources of Pope Francis' theology

MARKO IVAN RUPNIK: *According to the Spirit.* Spiritual theology on the move with Pope Francis' Church

ABBREVIATIONS

AL	*Amoris Laetitia*
CCC	*Catechism of the Catholic Church*
DCE	*Deus Caritas Est*
EG	*Evangelii Gaudium*
EN	*Evangelii Nuntiandi*
FC	*Familiaris Consortio*
LF	*Lumen Fidei*
LG	*Lumen Gentium*
LS	*Laudato Si'*
MeM	*Misericordia et Misera*
MV	*Misericordiae Vultus*
OT	*Optatam Totius*
VS	*Veritatis Splendor*

PREFACE TO THE SERIES

From the time of his first appearance in St Peter's Square on the evening of his election, it was more than clear that Francis' pontificate would be adopting a new style. His modest apparel, calling himself the Bishop of Rome, asking the people to pray for him – in the 'deafening silence' of a packed square – and greeting them with a simple '*buonasera*' (good evening) … these were all eloquent signs of the fact that there was a change taking place in the way the Pope related to people, and thus in the 'language' used.

The gestures and words that have followed from that occasion only confirm and strengthen this first impression. Indeed, it could be said that over the ensuing years, the image of the papacy has been decidedly transformed, involving a change that affects homilies, addresses and documents promulgated as well.

As could be predicted, this has generated divergent opinions, especially regarding his teaching. While many have in fact welcomed his magisterium with enthusiasm and deep interest, sensing the fresh wind of the Gospel, some others have approached it in a more detached way and, at times, with suspicion. There has been no lack of more absolute views, even going as far as to doubt the existence of a theology in Francis' teaching.

A summary judgement of this kind could come from the very different backgrounds of Francis and his predecessor, Benedict XVI. The latter, we know, has been one of the most outstanding and important theologians of the twentieth century and undoubtedly relied on his personal theological development in his rich papal magisterium. We have not yet fully appreciated, nor will we cease to appreciate, the depth of this magisterium. What Bergoglio has behind him, on the other hand, is his long and deep-rooted experience as a religious and a pastor.

However, this does not mean that his magisterium is without a theology. The fact that he was not mostly, or only, a 'professional' theologian does not mean that his magisterium is not supported by a theology. Were this the case, we could say that, strictly speaking, the majority of his predecessors were without a theology, given that Ratzinger represents the exception rather than the rule.

In any case, the fact that we can discuss the theological significance of Francis' magisterium, as well as the fact that, very often, some of his highly evocative and very immediate expressions have been so abused as to rob them of their profundity – in the journalistic as well as the ecclesial ambit – makes the response of this series, which I have the honour of presenting, a significant one.

By drawing on the competence and rigorous study of theologians of proven worth, coming from diverse contexts, the series has sought to research the theological thinking which supports the Pope's teaching. It explores its roots, its freshness, and its continuity with earlier magisterium.

The result can be found in the eleven volumes which make up this series with its simple and direct title: 'The Theology of Pope Francis'.

They can be read independently of one another, obviously; they have been written by individual authors independently of each other. Nevertheless, the hope is that a reading of the entire series would not only be a valuable aid for grasping the theology upon which Francis' teaching is based, in the various theological fields of knowledge, but also an introduction to the key points of his thinking and teaching overall.

The intention, then, is not one of 'apologetics', and even less so is it to add further voices to the many already speaking about the Pope. The aim is to try to see, and to help others to see, what theological thinking Francis bases himself on and expresses in such a fresh way in his teaching.

Among the many discoveries the reader could make in reading these volumes, one would certainly be to observe how so much of the beneficial freshness of the Council's teaching flows into Francis' magisterium. This is true both of the theological preparation he has had, and of what has followed from it. Given that it is perhaps still too soon for all this wealth to become common patrimony, peacefully and fully received by everyone, it should be no surprise that the Pope's teaching is sometimes not immediately understood by everyone.

By the same token, a point of no return has been reached in Francis' teaching, one that recent theology and the Council have both taught: that doctrine cannot be something extraneous to so-called pastoral theology and ministry. The truth that the Church is called to watch over is the truth of Christ's gospel, which needs to be communicated to the women and men of every time and place. This is why the task of the ecclesial magisterium must also be one of favouring this communication of the gospel. Hence, theology can never be reduced to a dry, desk-bound exercise, disconnected from the life of the people of God and its mission. This mission is that the women and men of every age encounter the perennial and inexhaustible freshness of Jesus' gospel.

Over these years there have been those who have heard some of Francis' own critical statements regarding theology or theologians, and have concluded that he holds it and them in low esteem. Perhaps a more detailed study of the Pope's teaching, such as offered by this series, could also be helpful for showing that, while we always need to be critical of a theology that loses its vital connection to the living faith of the Church, it is also essential to have a theology which takes up the task of thinking critically about this very faith, and doing so with 'creative fidelity', so that it may continue to be proclaimed.

Francis' teaching is certainly not lacking in a theology of this kind; and a theology of the kind is certainly one much desired by a magisterium such as his, which so wants God's mercy to continue to touch the minds and hearts of the women and men of our time.

Editor-in-chief
ROBERTO REPOLE

CONTENTS

Abbreviations 4
Preface to the series 5
Introductory Notes 11
   1. A theological style 11
   2. A theology of the Gospel 14
   3. A theology of the people of God 16

Chapter 1

Christian Love 19
   1. The source of love 21
   2. The experience of love 29
   3. Love as communion and mission 38

Chapter 2

Conjugal Love 51
   1. The truth of love 53
   2. The vitality of love 70
   3. The vulnerability of love 86

Chapter 3

Concluding summary 95
   1. The interpretation of Christian morality ... 96
   2. Appraisal of moral action 100
   3. Communicating moral theology 102

INTRODUCTORY NOTES

Preceded as it was by his predecessor's renunciation of the pontificate, the appearance on the ecclesial scene of the first non-European pope coming from 'almost the end of the world' was a genuine surprise.[1] The unusual choice of the name 'Francis', the familiar style of his first greeting: 'Brothers and sisters, *Buonasera*' (good evening), his presenting himself as 'Bishop of Rome', the request of the people to pray for him, asking to be blessed before he gave his blessing, all immediately revealed the new style of his pontificate.[2]

1. A theological style

If style can be described as 'a way of inhabiting the world,' consistent with 'giving shape' to all its elements and orienting them 'toward one of its essential parts,'[3] then Francis' style consists of presiding over ecclesial communion by fostering a 'new missionary "going forth"' by the Church (cf. *Evangelii Gaudium* 20-24, *EG*), that is 'capable of transforming everything, so that the Church's customs,

---

[1] A RICCARDI, *La sorpresa di papa Francesco. Crisi e futuro della chiesa* Mondadori, Milan, 2013.

[2] M GRONCHI – R REPOLE, *Il dolce stil nuovo di papa Francesco*, EMP, Padova, 2015.

[3] C THEOBALD, *Il cristianesimo come stile. Un modo di fare teologia nella postmodernità 1* (Nuovi Saggi Teologici 78), EDB, Bologna, 2009, 14-15.

ways of doing things, times and schedules, language and structures can be suitably channelled for the evangelization of today's world' (*EG* 27).

With regard to every ecclesial structure, the missionary transformation urged by Francis' style also includes theology, since 'the Church and theology exist to evangelize' (*EG* 133). How does Francis' ecclesial style challenge theological reflection? What is the theology that shines through his way of inhabiting the Church and guiding it through his magisterium?[4] And more specifically – corresponding to the intention of this book – which moral theology defines Francis' teaching?[5] Does it perhaps represent a major turning point?[6]

The question regarding the quality and moral theological value of Francis' magisterium requires that we first describe the peculiar nature of his theology. His first Encyclical, *Lumen Fidei* (*LF*), is illustrative in this regard, where he observes that theology 'is not just our discourse about God, but first and foremost the acceptance and the pursuit of a deeper understanding of the word which God speaks to us, the word which God speaks about himself.' Before being human discourse about God, theology is God's

---

4 A Cozzi – R Repole – G Piana, *Papa Francesco quale teologia?*, Cittadella, Assisi, 2016.
5 Fondazione Lanza (ed.), *Dove va la morale? Papa Francesco e il rinnovamento dell'etica* (Quaderni di etica Applicata), Proget. Albignasego (PD), 2016; P Carlotti, *La morale di papa Francesco*, EDB, Bologna, 2017).
6 S Goertz – C Witting, *Amoris Laetitia. Un punto di svolta per la teologia morale?* (L'Abside – Saggi di teologia 79), San Paolo, Cinisello Balsamo (MI), 2017.

discourse with human beings. God can become the 'object' of theological understanding only because he is the 'subject who makes himself known and perceived in an interpersonal relationship.'[7]

The distinction between the two aspects of theology, accepting and investigating the word of God, while it allows us on the one hand to imagine that these might be separate, on the other, suggests they be kept together. A moral theology that does not allow itself to be 'touched by God,' reducing itself to 'an effort of human reason to analyze and understand,'[8] would become merely 'a desk-bound theology' (*EG*, 133), 'a cold bureaucratic morality' (*Amoris Laetitia*, 312, *AL*), of no use and even a stumbling block for a Church in missionary 'going forth' mode.

The distinction between these two aspects of theology allows us to understand how it can take on different forms, corresponding to the extent to which it is close to lived experience, or worked out on the basis of a conceptual point of view. Theology is a unique discursive process with its source in the encounter with God and the reflective investigation which develops from this encounter. The theological process has varying degrees of development which correspond to the gradual critical understanding of lived experience of Christian faith.

---

7 Benedict XVI had almost completed a first draft of this encyclical: cf. Francis, *Lumen Fidei*, 29 June 2013, no. 7. All the magisterial documents cited in the text were taken from the *Acta Apostolicae Sedi*s and, if not yet published there, from the website: www.vatican.va.

8 *LF*, no. 36.

2. A theology of the Gospel

The way of inhabiting the Church and the world which shines through the words and gestures of Pope Francis envisages a theological form which is more keenly expressive of the essential content of the Gospel. Corresponding to the 'principle of *concordance between form and content*,'[9] his theology cannot be reduced to doctrinal teaching, and instead expresses a lifestyle.

The search for a discourse about God that is more vitally in contact with God's discourse with humankind is the tension which nurtures Francis' theology, not only in the area of homiletics and catechesis, but also at the most authoritative magisterial level, expressed in apostolic exhortations and encyclicals. If we describe the gospel as 'the fountain both of every saving truth, and discipline of morals,'[10] then Francis' theology is more a theology of the gospel which explores its vital foundation than a doctrinal theology which belongs to conceptual elaboration.

The gospel as understood by Francis is first of all the 'good and liberating message ... that has the listener confront a new situation and calls him or her to make a decision.'[11] The gospel is the *kerygma* that 'Jesus Christ loves

---

9 C THEOBALD, *Il cristianesimo come stile. Fare teologia nella post-modernità*, in Teologia 32 (2007 / 3), 280–303, 281.

10 Council of Trent, Decree concerning the Canonical Scriptures, in *The Council of Trent. The canons and decrees of the sacred and oecumenical Council of Trent*, Ed. and trans. J. Waterworth (London: Dolman, 1848).

11 W KASPER, *Papa Francesco – La rivoluzione della tenerezza e dell'amore. Radici teologiche e prospettive pastorali* (*Giornale di*

you; he gave his life to save you; and now he is living at your side every day to enlighten, strengthen and free you' (*EG* 164). Corresponding to the content of the evangelical *kerygma* there has to be a form of ecclesial proclamation which 'has to express God's saving love which precedes any moral and religious obligation on our part; it should not impose the truth but appeal to freedom; it should be marked by joy, encouragement, liveliness and a harmonious balance which will not reduce preaching to a few doctrines which are at times more philosophical than evangelical' (*EG* 165).

The theology that inspires the magisterium of Pope Francis, if we refer it to traditional ideas regarding moral teaching, could seem hard to define. But this is no reason for it to be less theological. In fact, to the extent that it aims more directly at capturing the word that God addresses to human beings in their concrete history, it presents as a more radical theology, in the sense that it is closer to the root which nourishes it. In Francis' theological style, what stands out more clearly is how the living word of God, resonant in the concrete life of human beings, inspires human words and aligns them properly as words about God. Indeed, theology is not a human logic by which we understand God, as a child would impress a shape in the sand on the seashore; rather is it the *logos* of God which radiates out in human form, just as a flower opens out and closes depending on the warmth of the sun.

Teologia 378), Queriniana, Brescia, 2015, 37. Also available in English as *Pope Francis' Revolution of Tenderness and Love, Theological and Pastoral Perspectives*, Paulist Press, 2015.

3. A theology of the people of God

The centrality of the proclamation of the gospel in Francis' teaching shapes it as more of a kerygmatic theology than a doctrinal one. Given the magisterium of his most immediate predecessors, who were much more into the theological development and definition of doctrine, Francis' magisterium could seem unconventional by comparison, even in conflict with them.[12] The apparent dissonance is such only if we misunderstand the different theological perspective of the Argentinian Pope, compared with the perspective shared by the European Popes, Wojtyla and Ratzinger. These latter, in the context of a Western world loosening itself from its Christian roots and redirecting itself toward moral relativism, urged a new evangelization, recalling the dependence of moral freedom on Christian truth[13] and pleading for recognition of the moral law inscribed within human nature.[14] Their theology was committed to discerning theological theories and comparing them with secular ideologies.

Pope Francis, anchored firmly in the Latin American world oppressed by social injustice and economic poverty, yearns for reconciliation and redemption from misery,

---

12 G Quaranta, 'Papa Francesco, la morale e il profumo del Vangelo', in Fondazione Lanza (ed.), *Dove va la morale? Papa Francesco e il rinnovamento dell'etica*, Proget, Padana, 2016, 25-40.

13 John Paul II, *Veritatis Splendor*, 6 August, 1993.

14 Benedict XVI, *Address to participants at the International Congress on the natural moral law, promoted by the Pontifical Lateran University*, Rome, 11 February, 2007; *Address to members of the International Theological Commission*, Vatican City, 5 October, 2007; *Address to the Federal Parliament*, Berlin, 22 September, 2011.

dreams of evangelization as the mandate 'to bring good news to the poor ... to let the oppressed go free, to proclaim the year of the Lord's favour' (*Lk* 4:18-19). His theology is a proclamation of mercy and the discernment of the concrete conditions of life that make it possible or not.

Francis' theology is not a school-based theology, but a theology of the people. An original expression of Argentinian theology, the theology of the people, albeit with similarities to the theology of liberation, socio-political and economic analysis often inspired by Marxism, prefers the historical analysis of culture and the popular ethos.[15] The originality of Argentinian theology, though specifying it in terms of Latin American theology on the one hand, anchors it within European theology on the other, either because Argentinian culture in general is influenced by European culture, or because of the familiarity of most Argentinian theologians with it, given that they have often been formed in the Old Continent in European philosophy and theology, especially French and German. More broadly speaking, the original Argentinian theology falls within the universal theological perspective promoted by Vatican Council II with its theology of the people of God (cf. *Lumen Gentium*, 9-17, *LG*) and its indications regarding the relationship between the Church and culture (cf. *Gaudium et Spes*, 53-62, *GS*).

The theology of the people of God, as an understanding of the Church's faith, shares the 'ecclesial form of faith'. Its elaboration is not the exclusive prerogative of certain individuals in the Church such as professional theologians, but is the activity of the 'believing subject which is the Church.' As a common ecclesial activity, theology is nevertheless a

---

15 W KASPER, *Pope Francis' Revolution of Tenderness and Love*, cit., 27-35.

differential activity in which the peculiar contribution of the magisterium of the pope and the bishops is to ensure 'our contact with the primordial source,' offering 'the certainty of attaining to the word of Christ in all its integrity.'[16] From an ecclesial perspective, the theological contribution of Francis corresponds properly to the apostolic charism, promoting rather than replacing the charism of theological ministry. This concept of the relationship between magisterial teaching and theological reflection is clearly attested to in *AL*, where Francis states that 'not all discussions of doctrinal, moral or pastoral issues need to be settled by interventions of the magisterium' (*AL 3*) and notes that 'the thinking of pastors and theologians, if faithful to the Church, honest, realistic and creative, will help us to achieve greater clarity' (*AL 2*).

With the intention of illustrating the worth of the moral theology which shines through the more relevant texts of Pope Francis' magisterium, the study which follows dedicates its first part to his teaching of a more fundamental nature, and the second part to the more specific teaching on married life. In pursuing this intention, there is not so much a presentation of all the ramifications of Francis' flourishing moral magisterium; instead, the sap which gives it life is highlighted. Hence the two parts focus respectively on Christian love as the vital essence of moral theology, and conjugal love as the fruitful core of family morality.

---

16 *LF*, no. 36.

Chapter 1
CHRISTIAN LOVE

Francis' theology, of a kerygmatic and pastoral nature, could seem distant from and not so relevant to the reflections contemporary moral theology has been engaging in.[1] In fact, it is precisely the difficult renewal of moral theology sought and guided by Vatican Council II that highlights the worth and focus of Pope Francis' teaching.

The renewal of contemporary moral theology can be noted as beginning with the Council's directive in *Optatam Totius* (*OT*) 16, giving it the task of shedding light, in more scientific and biblical terms, on 'the calling of the faithful in Christ and the obligation that is theirs of bearing fruit in charity for the life of the world.' Vatican Council II envisaged that moral theology would be a combined study of the relationship of the faithful with Christ and of their relationship with the world. Moral theology investigates the interweaving of these two relationships insofar as they are acts of human freedom,[2] studying, therefore, the nexus

---

1 A BONANDI, *Il difficile rinnovamento. Percorsi fondamentali della teologia morale postconciliare* (Questioni di etica teologica), Cittadella, Assisi, 2003.
2 Morality deals with the area of free action, at least action which has at least a minimal degree of awareness and voluntariness: 'Ibi incipit genus moris ubi primo dominium voluntatis invenitur': THOMAS AQUINAS, *Scriptum super Sententiis*, 1. 2, d. 24, q. 3, a. 2, c.

between the implementation of freedom, with regard to Christ, as in Christian faith, and the implementation of freedom with regard to the world, as in moral action.

The question of the relationship between Christian faith and moral action has marked the course of postconciliar moral theology, punctuated by the subsequent debates over the specific nature of Christian morality, the moral autonomy and ethics of faith, and what moral norms are based on.[3] The fundamental question of how the Christian faith influences moral action has been developed in the epistemological question of how faith and reason intervene in the recognition of moral content and, therefore, in the normative question of how faith and reason operate in the process of determining moral norms. One of the more critical post-conciliar issues which emerged immediately on publication of Paul VI's Encyclical *Humanae Vitae*, and which involved the growing tension between Christian faith and human reason, was the authority of the hierarchical Magisterium *in re morali* with respect to the competence of the individual conscience.

In the difficult search for an adequate solution to the fundamental question of the relationship between Christian faith and moral action, with its epistemological and normative implications, the papal magisterium recalled the essential condition of the 'unbreakable bond between faith

3 Among the more systematic and also analytic studies of the recent history of moral theology we note: B PETRA, 'Teologia morale', in G CANOBBIO – P CODA (eds), *La Teologia del XX secolo. Un bilancio. 3. Prospettive pratiche*, Città Nuova, Rome 2003, 97-193, 134-166.

and morality,'[4] cautioning against the risk of the 'serious and destructive dichotomy, that which separates faith from morality.'[5]

The critical understanding of the relationship between Christian faith and moral action constitutes the fundamental question of not just Catholic moral theology today, but also of Protestant and Orthodox theology.[6] The lead given by the principle resource, which can support the task of explaining the relationship between Christian faith and moral action, can be found in no. 16 of the Council Decree *OT*, which asked for the renewal of moral theology. Immediately prior to referring to this, the Decree indicates that, like the case of dogmatic theology, 'let the other theological disciplines be renewed through a more living contact with the mystery of Christ and the history of salvation.' It is precisely this 'living contact' with the saving mystery of Christ inhabiting human history that characterizes Francis' theology.

1. The source of love

'I never tire of repeating those words of Benedict XVI which take us to the very heart of the Gospel: "Being a Christian is not the result of an ethical choice or a lofty idea, but the encounter with an event, a person, which gives life a new horizon and a decisive direction" (*Deus Caritas Est*, 1, *DCE*).' Pope Francis' teaching is a decisive and heartfelt appeal for moral theology taught by the Church

4 JOHN PAUL II, *Veritatis Splendor*, 4.
5 *Ibidem*, 88.
6 B PETRA, *Teologia morale*, cit., 167.180.190.

to be authentically and effectively Christian, allowing every individual, all people to draw from 'the infinite love of God, who has revealed himself in Jesus Christ' (*EG* 7).

1.1 Personal encounter with Jesus

The personal encounter with Jesus Christ is an experience of love which finds its voice in the Gospel and is embodied in human relationships.

The experience of Jesus' love comes from hearing the Gospel, from 'lingering over its pages and reading it with the heart. If we approach it in this way, its beauty will amaze and constantly excite us' (*Evangelii Gaudium*, 264, *EG*.). The wonder and charm of Jesus' love, which the Gospel has spoken of, flows from the account of his mercy as it encounters human misery. Of considerable impact, for example, is the account of Jesus' encounter with the woman taken in adultery (Jn 8:1-11), and it is no accident that Francis suggested it as a concluding image for the celebration of the Extraordinary Jubilee of Mercy.[7] The woman's sin and the condemnation of the law which fill up the scene initially, are removed by Jesus who forgives the adulteress. In the silence of this scene, no longer cluttered by the pitiless judgement of the crowd, 'only two things: misery and mercy' remain – according to the touching expression of St Augustine.[8]

Jesus' love, as recounted by the Gospel, is embodied in human relationships. How that can happen is something

---

7 FRANCIS, *Misericordia et Misera* (*MeM*), 20 November 2016, Introduction.
8 AUGUSTINE, *In Evangelium Joannis* 33, 5.

Pope Francis has also pointedly spoken about. Way back on 21 September 1953, the day when the liturgy celebrates Mark the apostle and evangelist, the seventeen-year-old Jorge Bergoglio met Fr Carlos Duarte Obarra at his parish. Pope Francis vividly recalls going to him for confession and that 'I felt accepted by the mercy of God.' The depth of that personal experience is attested to by the way in which, the following year, the young Bergoglio reacted to the death of Fr Duarte Ibarra. When he came home after the funeral – Pope Francis tells us – 'I wept so much that evening, so much, hidden away in my room. Why? Because I had lost someone who made me feel God's mercy, that '*miserando atque eligendo*', an expression that I did not know at the time but which I chose for my episcopal motto … I like to translate *miserando* with a present participle that does not exist, 'mercying and choosing', to describe Jesus' gaze as he shows mercy and chooses, and takes someone to himself.'[9]

1.2 God's mercy

The experience of Jesus' love is the encounter with God's mercy. In fact, Jesus is 'the face of the Father's mercy,' he who 'by his words, his actions, and his entire person reveals

---

9 FRANCIS, *Il nome di Dio è Misericordia. Una conversazione con Andrea Torinelli*, Piemme, Milan, 2016, 26-27 (English edition, *The Name of God is Mercy*, Random House, 2016). The expression *miserando atque eligendo* is taken from ST BEDE THE VENERABLE, *Homily 21*, a commentary on the moment when Jesus calls the tax collector Matthew, seated at his tax bench, to follow him (cf. Mt 9:9).

the mercy of God.'[10] 'Everything in him speaks of mercy,'[11] which 'is always a gratuitous act of our heavenly Father, an unconditional and unmerited act of God.'[12]

A message both central to the Scriptures and overlooked by theological reflection,[13] mercy has been rediscovered for its importance by the recent magisterium of the Church, beginning with the memorable address at the opening of the Second Vatican Council, in which John XXIII directed the Church to prefer 'the medicine of mercy rather than of severity.'[14] The gold vein of mercy rediscovered by the Council was highlighted then by the magisterium of John Paul II, who investigated it in his second Encyclical, *Dives in Misericordia* (1980), and proposed establishing the Sunday after Easter as Divine Mercy Sunday, It was then highlighted by Benedict XVI who explored it in his first Encyclical *DCE* (2006), then presented it in social terms in his other Encyclical *Caritas in Veritate* (2009).

Mercy rediscovered and its meaning explored by the recent magisterial tradition, Pope Francis has placed it decisively at the heart of the Church's proclamation of the gospel, corresponding to its central place in the Old Testament, and more fully in the New Testament. For

10 FRANCIS, *Misericordiae Vultus (MV)*, 11 April, 2015, 1.
11 *Ibidem*, no. 8.
12 *MeM*, no. 2.
13 W KASPER, *Misericordia, Concetto fundamentale del vangelo – Chiave della vita cristiana* (Giornale di Teologia 361), Queriniana, Brescia, 2013. (English edition, *Mercy: The Essence of the Gospel and the Key to Christian Life*, Paulist Press, 2013).
14 JOHN XXIII, *Address at the solemn opening of the Council*, 11 October 1962.

Francis, 'The centrality of mercy ... represents Jesus' most important message.'[15] 'The Lord's strongest message.'[16] Hence, 'mercy' can be defined as the 'key word'[17] of his pontificate and theological programme.[18]

By establishing the centre of gravity of the gospel in mercy, Francis is putting the radical question of God to theology in a specific way.[19]

Classic theology and especially the theology of the manuals developed in our modern times, aimed at investigating the essential attributes of God beyond what has been revealed in the history of salvation. God's metaphysical essence, meaning the summary of his essential attributes, was then found in his Subsistent Being (*ipsum Esse subsistens*).

By scrutinizing the mystery of God in historical revelation in Christ, contemporary trinitarian theology finds its summary in charity: *DCE*, by considering God's free ways of acting rather than his metaphysical essence. The name which sums up all the attitudes adopted by God in the history of salvation is *Agápē*, revealing 'the love of someone

---

15 FRANCIS, *Il nome di Dio è Misericordia*, (*The Name of God is Mercy*), cit., 21.

16 *Ibidem*, 7.

17 W KASPER, *Papa Francesco – La rivoluzione della tenerezza e dell'amore*, (*Pope Francis' Revolution of Tenderness and Love* ...), cit., 49.

18 K APPEL – JH DEIBL (eds), *Barmherzigkeit und zärtliche Liebe. Das theologische Programm von Papst Franziskus*, Herder, Freiburg, 2016.

19 Cf W KASPER, *Papa Francesco – La rivoluzione della tenerezza e dell'amore*, (*Pope Francis' Revolution of Tenderness and Love* ...), cit., 55.

who dedicates himself to the other, whatever the other is like, even if the other does not deserve it, and this is because he finds within himself, and not in the other, the reason and strength for the movement that pushes him toward the other.'[20]

Within the succinct perspective of current trinitarian theology we discover Francis' specific theological outlook. He prioritizes mercy as as 'the first attribute of God', his very name.[21] Francis' point of view is that of someone who contemplates unconditional Love through the eyes of the poor, to whom God reveals himself as Mercy. Rather than considering Divine Love from the perspective of its *terminus a quo*, or as a wellspring of mercy for human beings, Francis considers it from the perspective of its *terminus ad quem*, or its being poured into their humanity in its wretchedness. Rather than being a theology from on high contemplating God in his gift of self, Francis' perspective is a theology from below which encounters God insofar as he reaches out to human beings in their wretchedness. In fact, 'mercy is the externally visible and effectively active aspect of the essence of God, who is love (1 Jn 4:8,16); it expresses the essence of God benignly disposed to the world and to human beings and constantly, historically filled with concern for them, he

---

20 L SERENTHÀ, *Gesù Cristo rivelatore del Padre*, Ut Unum Sint Centre, Rome, 1977, 86; A COZZI, *Manuale di dottrina trinitaria* (Nuovo Corso di Teologia Sistematica 4), Queriniana, Brescia, 2009, 944.

21 FRANCIS, *Il nome di Dio è Misericordia*, cit., 75. (*The Name of God is Mercy*). The title of the book in Italian, which we find on the frontispiece and cover, is in Pope Francis' own hand.

expresses his specific goodness and his specific love. Mercy is the "*caritas operativa et effectiva*" of God.'[22]

1.3 Mercy and misery

Mercy is the pouring out of God's love into human misery. In fact the Latin word *misericordia* indicates the heart (*cor*) addressed to the poor (*miseri*). Further more, it translates the two Hebrew words of the Old Testament *reḥem/raḥᵃmin* and *ḥesedh* and the Greek New Testament word *éleos*, which intend to express God's ineffable love for the human being in a wretched condition.[23]

The Hebrew word *reḥem/raḥamin* which specifically designates the 'bowels' and in the singular, the 'maternal womb', expresses in its translated form the loving, intimate, deep feeling binding two people such as the mother to her child (Ps 103:13; Jer 31:20) or brothers (Gen 43:30), which is spontaneously expressed in acts of compassion and forgiveness. This expression in an act of compassion of heart already introduces the meaning of the other Hebrew word *ḥesedh*, as well as the word *éleos* with which it is normally rendered in Greek. These two terms stress loving action rather than loving feeling, or in other words the conscious decision which arises out of fidelity, generally of someone superior toward their inferior, such as parents toward their

---

22 W Kasper, *Misericordia. Concetto fondamentale del vangelo*, cit., 136 (English edition, *Mercy: The Essence of the Gospel and the Key to Christian Life*, Paulist Press, 2013).

23 A Berlejung – C Frevel (eds), *I concetti teologici fondamentali dell'Antico e del Nuovo testamento* (*Biblioteca di Teologia Contemporanea* 143), Queriniana, Brescia, 2009, 476-469.

children, a sovereign toward his or her subjects, realized as merciful and compassionate kindness.[24] Mercy, as inferred by the words pointing to it, is both loving passion (*reḥem/raḥamin*) and action (*ḥesedh*, *éleos*). In terms of the more classic and authoritative theology of Augustine and Thomas, we would say that mercy is by nature affective and effective.[25]

Mercy is the most specific aspect that the love of God, *semper maior*, assumes in contact with the human condition, which can be labelled as wretched and miserable in a twofold sense – morally, and because we are creatures.

As creatures, our human condition is wretched because the human being, as a creature, is poor in terms of his or her own life. The human being exists and subsists only if and as long as he or she receives what is needed to live. Human beings owe their existence to others and so are fragile in themselves, since their life can diminish and be taken from them. By contrast to God, human beings are 'mortal'.

In a moral sense, human wretchedness is what human beings bring upon themselves. We are talking about evil, which depends on human responsibility, afflicting people through their own fault, what we properly consider to be sin. It is with regard to sinful misery that the Divine Mercy finds its highest expression. Mercy, which pervades all of Jesus' historical mission and earthly existence, reaches its greatest intensity when it is shown to sinners: 'Those who

24 A SISTI, 'Misericordia', in P. ROSSANO – G RAVASI – A GIRLANDA (eds), *Nuovo Dizionario di Teologia Biblica*, Edizioni Paoline, Cinisello Balsamo (MI), 1988. 978-984, 978.

25 W KASPER, *Misericordia. Concetto fondamentale del vangelo... (Mercy: The Essence of the Gospel and the Key to Christian Life)* cit., 40.

are well have no need of a physician, but those who are sick. Go and learn what this means, "I desire mercy, not sacrifice." For I have come to call not the righteous but sinners' (Mt 9:12-13). At the supreme and unrivalled moment of the revelation of God's merciful love, Jesus pours out his blood 'for the forgiveness of sins' (Mt 26:28).

Mercy for sinners is the supreme radiance of divine love, the imperious force of the wave which overrides the reef it encounters and irrepressibly submerges it. Mercy finds its greatest revelation in forgiveness, as 'the most visible sign of the Father's love, which Jesus sought to reveal by his entire life.'[26] Forgiveness is a *hyper*-merciful gift, the hyperbolic superabundance of a love that ransoms the human being from sinful misery 'seventy times seven' (Mt 18:22).

2. *The experience of love*

Divine Mercy arouses the experience of unconditional, undeserved and freely given love (cf. *Amoris Laetitia*, 296-297 *AL*) in the wretched individual, which surprises and attracts. Mercy surprises since it overshadows the equivalent logic of justice which, following the *tribuere unicuique suum* (to each his own), enjoins condemnation on the sinner. Mercy attracts since it corresponds to the superabundant logic of charity which, following the logic of the *dare omnibus gratis* (giving everything for nothing), forgives the sinner. Insofar as it overshadows justice and reveals charity, mercy represents 'the fullness of justice and the most radiant manifestation of God's truth' (*AL* 311). Therefore it is the

26 *MeM no. 2.*

'hermeneutic principle'[27] for understanding every other property of God in relation to human beings, as well as justice and divine truth.

2.1 The joy of love

The surprising experience of Divine Mercy, or in other words of a love that does not yield in the face of human misery, but which abounds in giving of itself freely, is an invitation to joy. It is on this joy that the emphasis of Pope Francis' magisterium falls. It is no coincidence that the word 'joy' recurs so frequently in his language[28] and is, significantly, the first noun to be found in *EG*[29] and *AL*.[30] For this purpose we need

---

27 W KASPER, *Papa Francesco – La rivoluzione della tenerezza e dell'amore*, (*Pope Francis' Revolution of Tenderness and Love* ...), cit., 54.

28 'The term "joy" (in its various forms: *alegría, gozo*) is one of the most frequent in the Bergoglian vocabulary. It is often qualified with adjectives like "new", "creative", "spiritual", "profound", "intimate", "immense", "irresistible", "eternal", "full", "eschatological" (Cf. JM BERGOGLIO, *In Lui solo la speranza. Esercizi spirituali ai vescovi spagnoli (15-22 January, 2006)*, Milan – Vatican City, Jaca Books – LEV, 2013, 74 ff., no. 2). He also dedicated some of his meditations in the retreat specifically to the joy of the Gospel (ID., *Aprite la mente al vostro cuore*, Milan, Rizzoli, 2013, 21-29)': A SPADARO, 'Amoris laetitia. Struttura e significato dell'Esortazione apostolica postsinodale di Papa Francesco', in FRANCESCO, *Amoris Laetitia. Esortazione postsinodale sull'amore nella famiglia*, (*Documenti ecclesiali*), Ancora, Milan, 2016. (the Australian edition, St Paul's Publications, 2016, of the Exhortation does not, of course, contain this commentary).

29 'The joy of the Gospel ...' (*EG 1*).

30 'The joy of Love ... ' (*AL*). Reference to joy also shines through his other authoritative document, the Encyclical *Laudato Si'*, from its very beginning.

to highlight how joy, as understood by Francis, cannot be reduced to an emotional and sentimental level, but concerns precisely the moral level of the experience of love. In classic terms of moral theology, there is a need to recognize how joy is not to be relegated to the 'passions', but should be ascribed among 'actions'. The joy felt by a person, which follows upon the act of rejoicing, is the result of the person enjoying God's love. The Latin verb *frui* is employed in the more classical theological tradition to stand for the specific nature of joyful activity. According to Augustine, then Thomas, the verb *frui*, to enjoy a thing, 'is to rest with satisfaction in it for its own sake.'[31] Anything but being selfish, the verb *frui* is rather an 'other-centred' activity, since its attractive centre is to be found in another reality which is loved for itself. Joy, as understood by Francis, is 'the joy of the Gospel [that] fills the hearts and lives of all who encounter Jesus' (*EG* 1). Christian joy is about resting complacently in God's merciful love poured into human hearts (cf. Rom 5:5) through the Spirit, a life 'which has its source in the heart of the Risen Christ' (*EG* 2).

Joy (*gaudium*), spiritual in nature, is not the same as sensible pleasure (*delectatio*); however, given the spiritual and bodily nature of the human being, one does not exclude the other. Thus it is that the spiritual depth of joy is reflected in psycho-physical sensibility, reawakening a 'new form of emotion' and finding 'other sensible expressions' (*AL* 164). Sensible pleasure, insofar as it is an expression of the spiritual joy that comes from God's love, is distinct

---

[31] AUGUSTINE, *De Doctrina Christiana*, 1, 4; THOMAS AQUINAS, *Summa Theologiae*, I-II, 11, 1, sc.

from purely hedonistic pleasure, the measure of which is subjective desire regardless of any otherness. 'Joy is never in our power, and Pleasure often is.'[32]

Joy, assisted by God's mercy, is not the reflection of its impact on the human being as a passive object, but the effect owed to its acceptance by the human being as a subject and agent. The encounter of God's freely given love, freely accepted by the human being, remains an 'unfathomable'[33] 'unsolvable'[34] mystery. This mystery is an intertwining of God's unconditional mercy and real human responsibility, without revealing them. And even when God's mercy is given the first and last word, as in more recent theology, to the point of hoping that all people will be won over to the joy of the gospel,[35] one cannot exclude the decisive word of human freedom in relishing divine mercy. If God's omnipotent love were to be imposed on the human being, violating our freedom, it would cease to be love. 'It is proper to God's mercy that it does not ignore our human freedom. God counsels but does not force us; urges us but does not trample over us, nor does he do us violence. In fact, as

---

32 CS Lewis, *Surprised by Joy: The Shape of My Early Life*, Mariner Books 1966 (first published 1955).

33 W Kasper *Misericordia. Concetto fondamentale del vangelo* (*Mercy: The Essence of the Gospel and the Key to Christian Life*) cit., 169.

34 HU von Balthasar, *TeoLogica. Lo Spirito della Verità*, Jaca Books, Milan, 1992 (English edition, *Theo-Logic. The Spirit of Truth*, Ignatius Press, 2005), 193.

35 HU von Balthasar, *Was dürfen wir hoffen?*, Johannes, Einsiedeln, 1989; Id., *Kleiner Diskurs über die Hölle Apokatastasis*, Johannes, Einsiedeln, 2007.

Augustine states, God who created you without you will not save you without you.'³⁶

Though the way God wins human beings over to the joy of the gospel may be mysterious, it is clear on the other hand that it is joy which is the original experience of Christian life, and one which is the source of other experiences. Enjoyment of God's merciful love is the primary experience of Christian morality, which is 'not a form of stoicism', 'merely a practical philosophy or a catalogue of sins and faults,' and it is also more than 'self-denial' (*EG* 39). Christian morality is a 'morality of joy'.

2.2 The response of love

Christian moral action is joyful action. At the heart of Christian morality beats 'the beauty of the saving love of God made manifest in Jesus Christ' (*EG* 36), the proclamation of which 'invites us to respond to the God of love who saves us.' Christian morality proclaimed as 'the response of love' to God's merciful love is the truth that, if it were not at the core of the Church's moral teaching, would reduce this teaching to a 'house of cards' and deprive the gospel of its 'freshness' and its 'fragrance' (*EG* 39).

The view of Christian morality as the 'response of love' could be better specified by describing it as the response through love, with love and in love.

The response of love is first of all a 'response through love' because it is aroused by God's love as he offers himself

---

36 W Kasper *Misericordia. Concetto fondamentale del vangelo* (*Mercy: The Essence of the Gospel and the Key to Christian Life*) cit., 168.

to us. God who loves us first is the condition for the possibility of a response, loving or otherwise, by the human being. 'Human freedom is reawakened, in fact, in the area of our humanity encountering another freedom. Even more so, human freedom can only be decided in the face of God's free offering and with his help, if we want to accept this offer or reject it. Only when faced with God's free offer, and with his help, are we encouraged to say yes, even though we are not forced to do so.'[37]

The response of love is also a 'response with love' because God's love not only arouses the human response but configures it constantly as such. The human response to God's love does not in fact consist of the human being switching from being the object of divine love to being the subject, and God no longer being the subject but the object of human love. The loving relationship between God and the human being is not a shift from the activity of the One to the passivity of the other, but involves the loving activity of both simultaneously in the form of an initiative on the part of the former and the corresponding reception of that by the latter. To God's action corresponds human acceptance of being acted upon. Human love for God consists in accepting God's love. The constant gift of divine love continuously configures human love as a response.

The response of love, then, is a 'response in love'. Insofar as it is acceptance of God's love, human love for God is always pregnant with, expectant of this love. But just as pregnancy implies the expansion of the female womb as the

37 *Ibidem.*

embryo grows, so acceptance of God's love increases human love. By growing in acceptance of divine charity, 'so too does its capacity for an even greater increase'[38] 'Charity increases by addition'[39] such that 'it is yet more in its subject, which implies a greater radication in its subject.'[40]

The response of love to God's love given to believers in Christ through the Holy Spirit, is not a sudden and instantaneous 'yes'. In harmony with Johannine pneumatology, according to which the Spirit leads us to the fullness of truth in Christ (cf. Jn 16:13), and with Pauline pneumatology, according to which the Spirit transforms us 'from one degree of glory to another' in the same image (cf. 2 Cor 3:18), Francis too conceives of life in the Spirit and according to the Spirit as a journey which, though not seamless, implies various degrees of practice of merciful love. The Christian's love is a 'dynamic process ... one which advances gradually with the progressive integration of the gifts of God and the demands of His definitive and absolute love in the entire personal and social life of man.'[41] Growth in charity does not necessarily translate into its best practice, or in other words into a greater quantity of charitable acts or into their superior quality. Similar to the growth of a biological organism, which can vary in how it develops over time, with latent phases where it gathers the resources for

38 THOMAS AQUINAS, *Summa Theologiae*, II-II, 24, 7, quoted in *AL* 134.
39 *Ibidem*, II-II, 24, 5, c.
40 *Ibidem*, II-II, 24, 4, ad 3.
41 JOHN PAUL II, *Familiaris Consortio (FC)*, 22 November, 1981, no. 9.

growth, and phases of clear development, charity too can grow over time at varying rates.[42]

Such a dynamic process 'is not simply a fixed progression towards what is better,' but 'an event of freedom, and even a struggle between freedoms that are in mutual conflict, that is, according to the well-known expression of St Augustine, a conflict between two loves: the love of God to the point of disregarding self, and the love of self to the point of disregarding God.'[43] Personal sin and the social structures of sin which follow from it mean that the nature of the human journey through history is one of 'continuous, permanent conversion which, while requiring an interior detachment from every evil and an adherence to good in its fullness, is brought about concretely in steps which lead us ever forward.'[44]

The dynamic and dramatic concept of Christian life corresponds to human historicity. The human being is not a 'being' already prepared in advance to act, but a 'becoming' which is given to human action. The concept of the human being as a 'dynamic history' instead of being a 'static essence' is reflected in the Church's recent moral teaching. In John Paul II's Apostolic Exhortation *FC* he states: 'But man, who has been called to live God's wise and loving design in a responsible manner, is an historical being who day by day builds himself up through his many free decisions; and so he knows, loves and accomplishes moral good by stages of growth.'[45]

---

42 THOMAS AQUINAS, *Summa Theologiae*, II-II, 24, 6, c.
43 *FC*, no. 6.
44 *Ibidem*, no. 9.
45 *Ibidem*, no. 34.

Following up recent magisterial tradition, Francis inserts an innovative development. By picking up on a category that the Second Vatican Council had coined, when speaking of ecumenism, for the 'purity of Catholic doctrine,'[46] Francis states that 'the hierarchy of truths' 'holds true as much for the dogmas of faith as for the whole corpus of the Church's teaching, including her moral teaching' (*EG 36*).

The hierarchy of truths is expressed, in the area of morality, through the hierarchy of virtues and their respective actions. At the top we find the virtue of charity through which faith carries out love for ones neighbour and it is no coincidence that this is suggested by the writers of the New Testament (cf. Rom 13:4, 10; Jas 2:8; Gal 5:14; 1 Thess 3:12) as the ultimate and most essential summary of the Christian moral message (*EG* 161). Anchored in the 'principle of the *primacy of grace*' (*EG* 112, 'which is mysteriously at work in each person, above and beyond their faults and failings' (*EG* 44), but also informed by the other principle by which *gratia non destruit, sed supponit et perficit naturam*, the traditional moral teaching of the Church teaches 'that anyone can have grace and charity, and yet falter in the exercise of the virtues because of persistent "contrary inclinations"' (*EG* 171). Given the dramatic and dynamic character of Christian life, 'Imputability and responsibility for an action can be diminished or even nullified by ignorance, inadvertence, duress, fear, habit, inordinate attachments, and other psychological or social factors' (*Catechism of the*

---

46 Vatican Council II, *Unitatis Redintegratio*, no. 11.

Catholic Church, 1735, *CCC*). While present in *habitu*, virtue cannot translate *in actu* due to involuntary conditioning. That explains why the Gospel recommends that we 'correct others and to help them to grow on the basis of a recognition of the objective evil of their actions (cf. Mt 18:15), but without making judgements about their responsibility and culpability (cf. Mt 7:1; Lk 6:37)' (*EG* 172).

While always looking to 'the attractiveness and the ideal of a life of wisdom, self-fulfilment and enrichment' (*EG* 168) or in other words, good that is desirable and which corresponds to the charity of Christ, Christians grow in love to the extent to which they risk discernment of what good is possible, bearing in mind the particular context and its limits (cf. *EG* 45).

3. *Love as communion and mission*

Gradual and dramatic loving correspondence to God's merciful love 'blossoms into an enriching friendship' (*EG* 8), the friendship of the human being with God which takes the name 'charity' according to the original notion of Thomas Aquinas, which was innovative for the time.

3.1 Love of God and neighbour

Aquinas' notion of charity as friendship underscores the part it plays for the human being, given that friendship is based on a 'communication of life (*super aliqua communicatione*).'[47] Charity comes from God and is infused in the human being, involving us in his own vitality. Communion with God

---

47 THOMAS AQUINAS, *Summa Theologiae*, II-II, 23, 1, c.

allows the human being to share in trinitarian communion, which can be thought of, according to the classic category of 'perichoresis', as 'eternal mutual giving.'[48] Trinitarian reciprocity is not resolved in the relationship of giving between Father and Son, Son and Father, but contemplates the gift of the Spirit. Trinitarian communion is a 'mutual reciprocity', aimed at 'infinitely multiplying the very dynamic by which it is reciprocity.' Genuine reciprocity is 'open and effusive.'[49]

God's self-communication in the history of salvation is a sharing of the altruism of trinitarian communion with the human being.[50] 'No one can receive God in themselves by appropriating him, because God is by essence the transferal of what is proper to him on others, and he is "known" and "possessed" only when we expropriate and transfer to others what is proper to us.'[51] There are not two loves, therefore, love of God and love of neighbour, but only one love, the love of God, which involves human beings in love of neighbour.

Love of neighbour, as a human fruit of its theological roots, is doubly revealing. It reveals that the one who practises it is in communion of love with God, and in that sense is 'the clearest sign for discerning spiritual growth in response to God's completely free gift' (*EG* 179). It

48 A Cozzi, *Manuale di dottrina trinitaria*, cit., 809.
49 P Coda, *Dalla Trinità. L'avvento di Dio tra storia e profezia*, (Percorsi di Sophia 1), Città Nuova, Rome, 2011. 567.
50 A Cozzi, *Manuale di dottrina trinitaria*, cit., 875-877.
51 HU von Balthasar, *Gloria. Un'estetica teologica. Nuovo Patto* (Già e non ancora 16), Jaca Books, Milan, 1977, 359. (English edition, *The Glory of the Lord, a Theological Aesthetics Vol 7. Theology: A New Covenant*, Ignatius Press, 1990).

also reveals the very love of God to the one who practises it, such that 'When we live out a spirituality of drawing nearer to others and seeking their welfare, our hearts are opened wide to the Lord's greatest and most beautiful gifts. Whenever we encounter another person in love, we learn something new about God' (*EG* 272).

The more we correspond to God's love, the more we are driven to love others, akin to a swimmer who swims toward the centre of the river and is pulled more strongly along by the current toward the river's mouth. Benedict XVI gave a lucid explanation of this dynamic in the following terms: 'Love of God and love of neighbour are thus inseparable, they form a single commandment. But both live from the love of God who has loved us first. No longer is it a question, then, of a "commandment" imposed from without and calling for the impossible, but rather of a freely-bestowed experience of love from within, a love which by its very nature must then be shared with others.'[52]

Love is a 'challenge... "to go forth"' (*EG* 20) which God gives to those who believe in him. The mission is not the love of neighbour which Christians practise after dwelling in God's love, dividing our time between divine contemplation and action in the world. Due to our communion with God in Christ through the Spirit, though it demands 'great generosity' on our part, the mission is no 'heroic individual undertaking,' since it is 'first and foremost the Lord's work' (*EG* 12). Evangelization, then, does not occur as the

---

52   *DCE*, 25 December, 2005, no. 18.

fulfilment of a moral obligation, but as the sharing of a joy (cf. *EG* 14).

Joy is the enjoyment of mercy which makes us merciful. 'Mercy renews and redeems because it is the meeting of two hearts: the heart of God who comes to meet the human heart. The latter is warmed and healed by the former. Our hearts of stone become hearts of flesh (cf. Ezek 36:26) capable of love despite our sinfulness. I come to realize that I am truly a "new creation" (Gal 6:15): I am loved, therefore I exist; I am forgiven, therefore I am reborn; I have been shown mercy, therefore I have become a vessel of mercy.'[53]

The encounter with God's love in Christ Jesus makes no distinction between being a 'disciple' and being a 'missionary', but always makes us 'missionary disciples' (*EG* 120). This missionary concept of divine love shapes human identity in missionary terms, envisaging an anthropology by which 'I am a mission on this earth; that is the reason why I am here in this world' (*EG* 273). Missionary anthropology can be further described in terms of its transcendent, relational and moral aspects.

Missionary anthropology is a transcendent anthropology in the sense that the human being who is involved in God's love of neighbour is a self implying another self. 'We become fully human when we become more than human, when we let God bring us beyond ourselves in order to attain the fullest truth of our being' (*EG* 8).

---

53 *MeM*, no. 16.

Missionary anthropology, which transcends individualism, is a relational anthropology in the sense that the human being, essentially in relationship with the divine Other and other human beings, realizes him or herself in the gift of that self to God and neighbour.

Missionary anthropology, essentially relational, is a moral anthropology in the sense that it is the activity that goes on between beings in relationship, meaning the love that binds us to God and our neighbour.

3.2 The Church's missionary communion

The communion of human beings with God gives rise to communion among those who correspond to God's love. Divine love given and accepted is not simply 'an accumulation of small personal gestures to individuals in need, a kind of "charity à la carte"' (*EG* 180) but fosters and consolidates 'interpersonal bonds' (*EG* 67), generating 'a mystical fraternity, a contemplative fraternity. It is a fraternal love capable of seeing the sacred grandeur of our neighbour, of finding God in every human being, of tolerating the nuisances of life in common by clinging to the love of God, of opening the heart to divine love and seeking the happiness of others just as their heavenly Father does' (*EG* 92).[54]

The first effect of the communion of human beings with God is ecclesial communion. In fact the Church is the 'sign and instrument both of a very closely-knit union

---

54   C THEOBALD, *"Mystik der Fraternité". Kirche und Theologie in neuem Stil*, in K APPEL – JH DEIBL (eds), *Barmherzigkeit und zärtliche Liebe*, 21-38.

with God and of the unity of the whole human race.'⁵⁵ Transcending every historical and institutional expression of itself, necessary though they may be, the Church is 'a mystery rooted in the Trinity' (*EG* 111). The Church is the communion of love between God and human beings, a love that finds its fullness and unsurpassed expression in the love of Christ for his own. The Church is the communion of those who love 'as' Christ loved (cf. Jn 13:34; 15:12, 17). It can be understood as the historical effect of the loving attraction that Christ, by means of the Spirit, exercises universally: 'And I, when I am lifted up from the earth, will draw all people to myself' (Jn 12:32). The *ekklesía* is the call to trinitarian love that God, through his Son Jesus, and the Holy Spirit addresses to the human race.

The Church, which arises from and grows 'by attraction' (*EG* 15) to trinitarian love, suffers from the resistance of Christians who, subject as they are to the many temptations of 'selfishness and spiritual sloth' (*EG* 81-83), 'sterile pessimism' (*EG* 84-86), 'spiritual worldliness' (*EG* 93-97), 'warring among ourselves' (*EG* 98-101), risk 'the joy of evangelization' (*EG* 83), 'missionary enthusiasm' (*EG* 80), 'the ideal of fraternal love' (*EG* 101), and 'community' (*EG* 92) being stolen from them.

The antidote to these anti-ecclesial temptations lies in the same attraction that stirs the Church, in the Holy Spirit who is called on constantly and who 'helps us in our weakness' (Rom 8:23). Even though entrusting ourselves to the Holy Spirit can 'cause us to feel disoriented', since it is

---

55   Vatican Council II, *Lumen Gentium* (*LG*), no. 1.

'like being plunged into the deep and not knowing what we will find', 'there is no greater freedom than that of allowing oneself to be guided by the Holy Spirit, renouncing the attempt to plan and control everything to the last detail, and instead letting him enlighten, guide and direct us, leading us wherever he wills' (*EG* 280). The Holy Spirit is 'the soul of the Church called to proclaim the Gospel' (*EG* 261).

Loving communion with God is essentially a 'missionary communion' which Jesus revealed by establishing the Twelve 'to be with him, and to be sent out to proclaim the message' (Mk 3:14). For the apostles, this 'closeness to Jesus is part of a common journey' (*EG* 23). 'In union with Jesus, we seek what he seeks and we love what he loves' (*EG* 267), so that the 'passion for Jesus' is at the same time a 'passion for his people' (*EG* 268).

Intimacy with Jesus, which sees us sharing in God's love, also sees that we love our neighbour as he does. According to the Parable of the Good Samaritan, someone is not our neighbour because they correspond to some determined social, ethnic, religious characteristic, but because they become our neighbour through God's merciful love. And since mercy is love shown to the wretched and poor, merciful love, though it is to be shown 'to everyone without exception' (EG 48), favours the poorest and most wretched among human beings.

Given that there is a preferential place in God's heart for the poor, that 'for your sakes he became poor' (2 Cor 8:9), the Church's mission is characterized by 'the preferential option for the poor' (*EG* 200), and the Church itself must be 'poor for the poor' (*EG* 198). Francis' teaching in this regard is clear: 'When we read the Gospel we find a clear indication: not so much our friends and wealthy neighbours, but above all the poor and the sick, those who are usually despised and overlooked, "those who cannot repay you" (Lk 14:14). There can be no room for doubt or for explanations which weaken so clear a message. Today and always, "the poor are the privileged recipients of the Gospel", and the fact that it is freely preached to them is a sign of the kingdom that Jesus came to establish. We have to state, without mincing words, that there is an inseparable bond between our faith and the poor. May we never abandon them' (*EG* 48).

Though the Church's mission may not always reflect the beauty of the gospel, 'there is one sign which we should never lack: the option for those who are least, those whom society discards' (*EG* 195). Francis draws attention to 'those who are victims of various kinds of human trafficking' (*EG* 211); 'women who endure situations of exclusion, mistreatment and violence, since they are frequently less able to defend their rights'(*EG* 212); 'unborn children, the most defenceless and innocent among us. Nowadays efforts are made to deny them their human dignity and to do with them whatever one pleases, taking their lives and passing laws preventing anyone from standing in the way of this' (*EG* 213). Besides, by promoting 'an integral ecology,'[56] which shows how 'all creatures are connected,'[57] among the 'weak and defenceless beings who are frequently at the mercy of economic interests

56   FRANCIS, *Laudato Si'* (*LS*), 24 May, 2015, Ch. 4.
57   *Ibidem*, no. 42. There is an insistence in this Encyclical on

or indiscriminate exploitation' is 'creation as a whole' (*EG* 215). So merciful love hears 'both the cry of the earth and the cry of the poor.'[58]

Being close to 'new forms of poverty and vulnerability' (*EG* 210) leads to and requests a 'creativity of mercy,'[59] which gives new realism to the traditional works of mercy. 'The works of mercy are "handcrafted", in the sense that none of them is alike' (*MeM* 20).

3.3 The mission of communion in the world

The intimate connection between nature and culture,[60] which means that 'the human being is always situated in a culture' (*EG* 115) invites us to spell out the principle of the relationship between divine grace and human nature in cultural terms: *gratia non destruit, sed supponit et perficit culturam.*

Culture, understood as 'the lifestyle of a given society, the specific way in which its members relate to one another, to other creatures and to God' (*EG* 115), is the ground that the gospel fertilizes and transforms (*EG* 116). The *semina Verbi* sown by the Spirit in cultures have brought forth, for example, 'Christian humanism' (*EG* 68) in some peoples, especially in the West, and given rise to 'popular piety' (*EG* 68) amongst Catholic populations. The Holy Spirit's cultural

---

how 'everything is connected (91, 240), 'everything is interrelated' (92, 120, 142), 'everything is closely interrelated' (137), 'everything is interconnected' (117, 138).

58 *Ibidem*, no. 49.
59 *MeM* no. 18.
60 Cf. VATICAN COUNCIL II, *Gaudium et Spes*, no. 53

fertilization nourishes the *sensus fidei* of the baptized, helping them to discern the 'signs of the times' (cf. *EG* 119).

The Holy Spirit inscribes the gospel in every culture without identifying it with any one culture. By communicating the gospel as something inculturated yet transcultural, the Holy Spirit moulds the one, catholic Church, united in love and different in its expressions. 'The same Spirit is that harmony, just as he is the bond of love between the Father and the Son. It is he who brings forth a rich variety of gifts, while at the same time creating a unity which is never uniformity but a multifaceted and inviting harmony' (*EG* 117).

The work of the Spirit in bringing the many kinds of culture into the harmony of unity, is the beginning of social love which is 'one of the highest forms of charity', concerned not only with 'micro-relationships' between friends, families, small groups, but also 'macro-relationships' of a social and political kind (*EG* 205).

The Church's mission to assist the Holy Spirit's sowing, is to 'promote a culture of mercy'[61] and a civilization of love by promoting the common good and peace in society. (*EG* 217-237). Developing the Social Doctrine of the Church, whose pillars remain 'the primary and fundamental parameters of reference for interpreting and evaluating social phenomena,' Francis proposes 'four specific principles which can guide the development of life in society' (*EG* 221).

The first principle, bearing in mind the tension between the fullness of time as the horizon which constantly opens

61 *MeM*, no. 20.

before us, and limitation of the moment, which occupies a circumscribed space, states that 'time is greater than space' (*EG* 222). 'Giving priority to time means being concerned about *initiating processes rather than possessing spaces*' (*EG* 223), and enables us to escape 'being obsessed by immediate results,' allowing us 'to work slowly but surely' (*EG* 223).

The second principle, stating that 'unity prevails over conflict' (*EG* 228), invites us to accept and put up with tensions and oppositions, without reductionism or syncretism. In fact conflict can become 'a link in the chain of a new process' (*EG* 227) aimed at a 'diversified and life-giving unity' which 'preserves what is valid and useful on both sides' (*EG* 228).

The third principle, maintaining that 'realities are more important than ideas' (*EG* 231), leads to fleeing from 'ineffectual forms of idealism and nominalism capable at most of classifying and defining, but certainly not calling to action' (*EG* 232). Proclamation of the gospel calls on 'the principle of the incarnation of the Word and its being put into practice' (*EG* 233).

The fourth criterion, recalling that 'the whole is greater than the part' (*EG* 237), urges us not to 'be obsessed with limited and particular questions,' losing sight of 'the totality or integrity of the Gospel' (*EG* 237). The superiority of the whole over the parts does not have the sphere as its model 'where every point is equidistant from the centre, and there are no differences between them.' Reference is rather to 'the polyhedron, which reflects the convergence of all its parts, each of which preserves its distinctiveness' (*EG* 236). What resists the work of the Spirit inscribing loving goodness in social culture and social institutions, is unloving evil, and this is reflected in the social structure. This evil resistance to social love shows up in the 'throwaway culture.'[62] As a result of the 'dominant technocratic paradigm,'[63] it encourages an 'economy of exclusion' (*EG* 53-54) and 'an idolatry of money' (*EG* 55-56), hotbeds of inequality[64] and violence (cf. *EG* 59-60). This 'deterioration of ethics' (*EG* 64) is the effect and at the same time the cause of a notion of the human being caught up in 'extreme individualism' (*AL* 133) where other human beings are concerned, and 'tyrannical anthropocentrism'(*LS* 68) unconcerned with other creatures.

The 'evangelical discernment' of the signs of the times, aimed at distinguishing 'what might be a fruit of the kingdom from what runs counter to God's plan' (*EG* 5'), or in other words what is good according to the Spirit and what is the evil that runs counter to it, trusts in the 'infinite creativity' of the Holy Spirit who 'knows how to loosen the knots of human affairs, including the most complex and inscrutable' where 'many of the things we think of as evils, dangers or sources of suffering, are in reality part of the pains of childbirth which he uses to draw us into the act of cooperation with the Creator' (*LS* 80). The work of the Holy Spirit continues God's creative action.

62 *LS* no. 22.
63 *Ibidem*, no. 101.
64 The Italian term '*inequità*' is a neologism of Francis, translated into English as 'inequality' rather than 'inequity'. But in Italian, it also suggests a play on the word '*iniquità*' (iniquity), resulting from the lack of '*equità*'.

Chapter 2
CONJUGAL LOVE

Francis' magisterium, of which *Evangelii Gaudium* is the *magna carta*, finds its first great expression in *Amoris Laetitia* (*AL*), the post-synodal Apostolic Exhortation on love in the family. The moral theology envisaged by *EG*, therefore, also finds a place in the family ethics laid out in *AL*. Furthermore, what we find there not only expresses but develops Francis' moral magisterium, similar to a shoot which extends and enriches the vine while being nourished by it.

The text of the Exhortation is literally a *textus*, the result of the threading together of many and varied contributions provided by the synodal process which preceded it, which was something new for the extent of ecclesial involvement it had and for being spread over two Assemblies of bishops, an extraordinary one in October 2014[1] and an ordinary one in October 2015.[2] The synodal character of *AL* is evidence of traditional continuity and renewed interpretation of the family ethics fostered by Pope Francis.

---

1 L Baldisseri (ed.), *Le sfide pastorali sulla famiglia nel contesto dell'evangelizzazione. III Assemblea Generale Straordinaria del Sinodo dei Vescovi*, Libreria Editrice Vaticana, Vatican City, 2015.

2 L Baldisseri (ed.), *La vocazione e la missione della famiglia nella Chiesa e nel mondo contemporaneo. XIV Assemblea Generale Straordinaria del Sinodo dei Vescovi*, Libreria Editrice Vaticana, Vatican City, 2016.

AL properly revolves around 'love in the family' as the complete title suggests. By focusing attention on love in the family, Francis puts conciliar and post-conciliar teaching to good use.³ This renewed a two-thousand-year-old tradition regarding the purpose of marriage as being the realisation of certain goods, primarily procreation, in love understood in Christian terms as the mutual gift of life by the couple. This establishes the meaning of human sexuality and the essence of matrimony.⁴

The novelty of Francis' contribution is to consider the event of love given and commanded by Christ in the reality of family life. The belief that supports and refines his outlook is that the concrete history of families is a *locus theologicus*, a human place in which the mystery of God's love can be known. 'We do well', writes Francis, picking up *Familiaris Consortio* (*FG*) and through it *Gaudium et Spes* (*GS*), 'to focus on concrete realities, since "the call and the demands of the Spirit resound in the events of history", and through these "the Church can also be guided to a more profound understanding of the inexhaustible mystery of marriage and the family"' (*AL* 31). The gospel of marriage and the family is sown in the love experienced and nurtured daily between spouses and between parents and children (cf. *AL* 96).

---

3 G Marengo, *Generare nell'amore. La missione della famiglia cristiana nell'insegnamento ecclesiale del Vaticano II a oggi* (in Teologia Saggi), Citadella, Assisi, 2014.

4 A Fumagalli, *L'amore sessuale. Fondamenti e criteri teologico-morali* (in the *Biblioteca di Teologia Contemporanea* 182), Queriniana, Brescia 2017, 301-357.

The gospel of marriage and the family is not another gospel compared with the proclamation of God's saving love as manifested in Jesus Christ, which first of all invites us to respond to the God who loves and saves us. Marriage and the family, from the gospel's point of view, are also a response of love and to God's love. This central Christian truth is placed at the heart of *AL*, in the fourth and fifth chapters dedicated to *Love in marriage* and *Love made fruitful*, which Francis indicates explicitly as the 'two central chapters' (*AL* 6) of the Exhortation. Conjugal love understood as a loving response to Christ's love is the essential truth of the matrimonial and family morality outlined in *AL* and, more generally, envisaged by the teaching of Pope Bergoglio.[5]

According to the logic to be found in *AL*, the response of conjugal love to God's love must be understood in its truth, in its dynamics and in its vulnerability.

1. The truth of love

True conjugal love corresponds to God's love revealed in Christ and is made real by the Spirit.

1.1 Conjugal love

Conjugal love is the reflection of Christ's love in the love between the couple. In the succinct definition proposed by

---

5 POPE FRANCIS, *La famiglia genera il mondo. Le catechesi del mercoledì.* 10 December 2014 – 16 September (Famiglia e Vita 8), Libreria Editrice Vaticana, Vatican City, 2015. (The catechesis on the family, which began this day, Wednesday 10 December 2014 and continued on subsequent Wednesdays, can be found on the Holy See's website).

Francis, it is an '"affective union", spiritual and sacrificial, which combines the warmth of friendship and erotic passion' (*AL* 120). Conjugal love is harmonious integration, in the 'spiritual and sacrificial' dimension, of another two dimensions of love, the friendly and the erotic. This threefold dimension of conjugal love is indicated by the classic terms *agape*, *philia* and *eros*.[6]

LOVE AS EROTIC, FRIENDLY AND AGAPAIC LOVE

Conjugal love is erotic love. The erotic dimension brings to conjugal love the pyhysical and psychological experience of the man and woman, or in other words 'desires, feelings, emotions' or what the ancients called the 'passions' (*AL* 143), and the physical expressions of love found in a caress, an embrace, a kiss, and sexual union (cf. *AL* 157). The erotic dimension characterizes conjugal love as 'passionate' and 'sexual' love. Loving passion, which arises 'whenever "another" becomes present and part of a person's life,' generates the 'tendency' to reach out (*AL* 143) to the other. Passionate feelings arouse sexual attraction which, in turn, feeds passionate feelings.

Recently, magisterial teaching has removed the negative baggage which has weighed upon sexual experience, on the passions, for much of the Church's history, not just outside but also within marriage.[7] Sensitized by instances of so-

---

[6] Cf. X. LACROIX, *Les mirages de l'amour*, Bayard, Paris 1997, 77-108; JM MORILLA DELGADO (ed.), *Eros, philia, agape. Le declinazioni dell'amore*, Lombar Key, Bologna, 2008.

[7] M PELAJA – L SCARAFFIA, *Due in una carne. Chiesa e sessualità nella storia* (in *Storia e società*), Laterza, Rome – Bari, 2008.

called 'personalism', teaching on marriage, especially since the Second Vatican Council, has recognized the positive value of the erotic dimension in conjugal love. All of John Paul II's teaching, and especially his catechesis on human love, document in a profound way how this censure has been overcome, along with the mere tolerance of erotic love. His teaching and catechesis attest to the considerable appreciation given the sexualized body and sexual pleasure.[8]

By recalling John Paul II's catechesis, Francis decisively excludes the idea that 'we consider the erotic dimension of love simply as a permissible evil or a burden to be tolerated for the good of the family.' On the contrary, he invites us to appreciate it as a 'gift from God' (*AL* 152), as 'a marvellous gift' (*AL* 150) of the Creator to his creatures.

Other than being erotic, conjugal love is a love of friendship. 'After the love that unites us to God, conjugal love is the "greatest form of friendship" (*AL* 123), Francis states, quoting Thomas Aquinas.[9]

In order to better describe friendship, it is appropriate to distinguish, as Aristotle teaches, genuine friendship from merely useful or pleasurable friendships, the kind where the other is liked because we gain some usefulness or pleasure for ourselves from this friendship.[10] Genuine friends are

---

8 JOHN PAUL II, *Uomo e donna lo creò. Catechesi sull'amore umano*, Città Nuova – Libreria Editrice Vaticana, Rome, 1992 (also available in English as *Man and Woman He Created Them: A Theology of the Body*, Pauline Books and Media, 2006).

9 THOMAS AQUINAS, *Summa contra Gentiles*, III, 123, 6.

10 ARISTOTLE, *Nicomachean Ethics*, VIII, 3, 1156a (ed. Bywater, Oxford, 1984); cf. THOMAS AQUINAS, *Summa Theologiae*,

'those who wish well to their friends for their sake.'[11] In the love of friendship I wish the other well for the other's sake.[12]

The difference between erotic desire and friendly benevolence depends on the different involvement of personal freedom. In erotic desire, personal freedom is more a spectator than an actor. It is primarily the psychological and physical dynamics at work, such as the senses and feelings. The individual feels attracted, affected, made emotional, seduced. In friendly benevolence, personal freedom takes a more decisive initiative; it is the human spirit which is mainly at work here. Friendship arises from free choice and persists when it is nurtured. In the classic terms of philosophy and theology, while erotic desire is a passion (*páthos*), friendly benevolence is a virtue (*héxis, habitus*).[13]

Friendship between spouses, 'born of a shared life,' is different from other forms of friendship inasmuch as it pursues 'an indissoluble exclusivity expressed in the stable commitment to share and shape together the whole of life' (*AL* 123).

Beyond eroticism and friendship, conjugal love is agapaic love, in other words a spiritual and sacrificial love: spiritual because it comes from the Holy Spirit who pours the divine *agape* into the hearts of men and women believers (cf. Rom 5:5); sacrificial because it disposes the spouses for the gift of their own life for the other, loving each other as

---

I-II, 26, 4, ad. 3.
  11   ARISTOTLE, *Nicomachean Ethics*, VIII, 3, 1156b.
  12   THOMAS AQUINAS, *Summa Theologiae*, I-II, 26, 4.
  13   ARISTOTLE, *Nicomachean Ethics*, VIII, 1, 1155a.

Christ loved (cf. *AL* 120). Agapaic love is love freely given, the grace of the Holy Spirit who enables the spouses to give themselves to each other.

This gratuitousness of agapaic love adds a 'certain perfection' to the love of friendship. The contemplative gaze on the other as 'ends in themselves' (*AL* 128), the recognition of the other's 'great worth' are such because *agape* not only seeks the other's good but seeks it also when the other has become 'no longer physically appealing but intrusive and annoying' (*AL* 127). Agapaic love is the freely given gift of self even when the friend becomes an enemy. *Agape* is love 'that never gives up' (*AL* 119), love which puts up with the unbearable. The gratuitousness of agapaic love exceeds the mutuality of the love of friendship: charity 'consists in loving rather than in being loved.'[14]

Eros, *philia* and *agape* are three dimensions of true love. True love, or conjugal charity, is desire for the other, friendship with the other, gift of self for the other. The dimensions of conjugal love, charity, which is erotic, friendly and agapaic, are intrinsically related, as a result of the mutual interaction between desire and friendship, friendship and charity, charity and desire.

The interaction of erotic, friendly, agapaic love

Erotic, passionate and sexual desire features emotion and promise. Eros is 'e-motion' in the sense in which it moves out of itself towards the other, with the need, even the covetous need, to join with the other. *Eros* is also 'pro-mise',

14   Thomas Aquinas, *Summa Theologiae, I-II, 27, 1.*

in the sense in which it let us glimpse union with the other as something salutary.

Erotic desire typically means falling in love. Falling in love is love in a *statu nascenti*, electrified by the prospect of an entire life happily in love. Sensual attraction and the feelings of affection between the lovers invoke the 'again' and the 'more' of a lasting and fulfilling love. 'Lovers do not see their relationship as merely temporary,' observes Francis, inviting us to recognise 'the signs that this is the case' (*AL* 123).

As much as it is related to conjugal love, falling in love does not coincide with it: it can lead to it, revive it, facilitate it, but it is not the same, since conjugal love contemplates benevolent friendship. Friendship contributes the more specific personal dimension of love to sensual and sentimental infatuation, so the other does not only please and attract, but is consciously and willingly chosen. Conjugal friendship personalizes erotic desire, avoiding its possible reduction to a merely physical instinct or just a psychological impulse, valuing it for its properly human quality.

The personalization of erotic desire allows it to disclose its character as a manifestation, aside from the two features of emotion and promise already indicated. 'If passion accompanies a free act, Francis notes, 'it can manifest the depth of that act' (*AL* 146). The goodness of conjugal friendship shines out in erotic desire.

Erotic desire and personal friendship are peculiar dimensions of conjugal love, the harmony of which, however, can never be taken for granted. *AL*'s healthy realism reminds us that 'our human equilibrium is fragile; there is a part of us that resists real human growth, and any moment it can unleash the most primitive and selfish tendencies' (*AL* 157). Unbalanced forms of conjugal love find their common root in the depersonalization of erotic desire, that is, no longer experienced within the context of personal friendship.

Experienced in Christ, 'Conjugal love reaches that fullness to which it is interiorly ordained: conjugal charity' (*AL* 120). Conjugal love, both erotic and friendly, is fully realized when it becomes agapaic love. Desire for the other, which belongs to *eros*, and the good of the other, which belongs to *philia*, find their completion through the gift of self, which belongs to *agape*.

Agape, given freely by the Holy Spirit, does not represent a choice of conjugal love, for which *eros* and *philia* would be sufficient, but the necessary condition for it not to diminish and indeed for it to increase. The promise of great love without end, as much as it is disclosed by erotic desire and pursued by benevolent friendship, challenges those in love and married couples, who have to take account of their personal weakness,[15] today fed by a social climate which is considerably conditioned by individualism (cf. *AL* 33), a 'culture of the ephemeral' (cf. *AL* 39) and political agendas (*AL* 44).

The fragility of conjugal friendship, as well as of erotic desire, shows us that true, full and lasting love is 'a plan

---

15   G Cucci, 'La coppia e la sfida del tempo', *Amoris laetitia. Esortazione apostolica postsinodale sull'amore nella famiglia. Testo integrale e commento de "La Civiltà Cattolica"* (Crocevia), Ancora, Milan, 2016, 271-287.

bigger than our own ideas and undertakings' (*AL* 124), a plan that cannot be realized 'without a great mystery'. So that erotic and friendly conjugal love can 'overcome all trials' and 'remain faithful in the face of everything, it needs the gift of grace to strengthen and elevate it' (*AL* 124). The enduring of crises as part of conjugal love, as well as its fulfilment, demand an energy that spouses cannot produce of their own accord. Without *agape*, *philia* and *eros*, they stumble and fail.

What is realistically impossible on the basis of *philia* and *eros*, becomes a real possibility with the gift of *agape*. Agapaic love strengthens conjugal friendship, so that wishing the other's good becomes gift of self for the other. By healing moral fragility and overcoming the limits of a man and a woman as the creatures they are, the gift of *agape* strengthens their friendship to the extent of it becoming conjugal charity. Agapaic love, by fortifying and enabling conjugal friendship, increases their benevolence toward the other, the readiness to want what is good for the other. This reawakens feelings and sensitivity, nurturing erotic desire.[16]

If, on the one hand, divine, agapaic love enables conjugal, friendly and erotic love, on the other, conjugal love enables divine love, allowing it to show itself in human terms. Not only does *agape* nurture *philia* and *eros* as well, but *eros* and *philia* enrich *agape*. The enrichment of *agape* by *eros*, especially, is something Francis considers to be essential both for love to be true and for its witness value.

---

16 J Bastaire, *Eros redento. Amore e ascesi*, Qiqajon, Magnano (VC), 1991.

With regard to the truth of love, Francis takes up the legacy of Benedict XVI whose appreciation of erotic love allows him to state that 'man cannot live by oblative, descending love alone. He cannot always give, he must also receive. Anyone who wishes to give love must also receive love as a gift.'[17] If it is in fact true that *eros* without *agape* degrades to 'pure "sex"', becoming 'a mere "thing" to be bought and sold,'[18] it is likewise true that *agape* without *eros* is locked into becoming 'a world apart, admirable perhaps, but decisively cut off from the complex fabric of human life.'[19] Echoing his predecessor, Francis reminds us that 'authentic love also needs to be able to receive the other, to accept one's own vulnerability and needs, and to welcome with sincere and joyful gratitude the physical expressions of love found in a caress, an embrace, a kiss and sexual union.' (*AL* 157).

Concerning the witness value of true love, by considering the common teaching of the mystics, according to which divine love finds its privileged expression symbolized by the love of spouses more than by other forms, Francis notes that 'a love lacking either pleasure or passion is insufficient to symbolize the union of the human heart with God'(*AL* 142).

1.2 Christian marriage

Conjugal charity, which would not exist without friendly and erotic love, is specifically and fully configured only by agapaic love. Agapaic love is not superfluous nor optional by

17 BENEDICT XVI, *Deus Caritas Est, DCE*, no. 7.
18 *Ibidem*, no. 5.
19 *Ibidem*, no. 7.

comparison with friendly and erotic love. So that conjugal love can achieve its vital 'love them to the end' character, (Jn 13:1), it needs *agape*. Also true for conjugal love is Paul's teaching wherein if there is no *agape*, then nothing else will do (cf. 1 Cor 13:3).

The enhancement of conjugal love in conjugal charity is what motivates proclamation of the 'Gospel of the family' (*AL* 60),[20] which envisages marriage as a 'gift' (*AL* 61) of the Lord and a 'vocation', or 'a response to the specific call to live conjugal love.' The gift and vocation of marriage are proclaimed by the Gospel of the family in reference to the sacrament of marriage conceived of not as 'a social convention, an empty ritual or merely the outward sign of a commitment,' but a 'real representation' of the 'same relationship between Christ and the Church' (*AL* 72).

SACRAMENTAL SIGNIFICANCE

By adding in the more classic definition of the sacraments as 'efficacious signs of grace,'[21] Francis describes the sacrament of marriage as 'a precious sign'. The preciousness of sacramental marriage consists in it becoming 'the icon of God's love for us', such that in the union of the spouses the communion of the three Divine Persons 'is mirrored' and Christ's love for his Church is made 'visible'. (*AL* 121).

This qualification of the sacrament of marriage as a 'precious sign' needs to be added to the other one, that it is an

---

20 W KASPER, *Il vangelo della famiglia* (*Giornale di Teologia* 371), Queriniana, Brescia, 2014 (also in English as *The Gospel of the Family*, Paulist Press, 2014.)

21 *Catechism of the Catholic Church, CCC,* no. 1131.

'imperfect sign of the love between Christ and the Church' (*AL* 72). There is an 'imperfect' analogy between the 'human couple of husband and wife and Christ and his Church' (*AL* 73). The imperfection of marriage compared to Christ's love depends on its place in the history of salvation, since it is a dramatic and gradual reality which takes place over time and involves human freedom.

The peculiar nature of the sacramental sign of marriage finds further illustration in comparison with virginity. These two states of life, beyond any question of one being inferior or superior to other, 'complement one another, and consequently ... some can be more perfect in one way and others in another' (*AL* 159). Virginity and marriage are two specific Christian signs: 'Whereas virginity is an "eschatological" sign of the risen Christ, marriage is a "historical" sign ... of the earthly Christ' (*AL* 161). The eschatological sign of virginity indicates the 'the coming of the Kingdom and the need for complete devotion to the cause of the Gospel (cf. 1 Cor 7:32). It is also a reflection of the fullness of heaven, where "they neither marry not are given in marriage"' (*AL* 159). The historical sign of marriage 'manifests the closeness of God who is a part of every human life, since he became one with us through his incarnation, death and resurrection' (*AL* 161).

As a sacrament, marriage is more than a sign of grace; it is a real sign. 'Christian marriage is a sign of how much Christ loved his Church in the covenant sealed on the cross, yet it also makes that love present in the communion of the spouses' (*AL* 73). In such a way, sexual union and the entire network of relationships which spouses weave between them with their children and the world around them, 'will be steeped in and strengthened by the grace of the sacrament. For the sacrament of marriage flows from the incarnation and the paschal mystery' (*AL* 74). The sacrament sees that the goods which are constitutive of marriage – faithfulness and openness to new life – are 'commitments that can be better kept through the help of the grace of the sacrament' (*AL* 73).

Sustained by sacramental grace, marriage as an institution, with its obligatory properties of unity and indissolubility, is not something external to conjugal love, like an external scaffolding which supports it in the best of cases or smothers it in the worst case scenario. The institution of marriage appears rather to be the intrinsic requirement of conjugal love to manifest itself to the world around it and throughout the course of history. Faced with the widespread attempts to make marriage 'a purely private affair,' reducing it to 'a mere spontaneous association for mutual gratification,' 'choosing to give marriage a visible form in society by undertaking certain commitments shows how important it is' (*AL* 131).

Full ideal

According to *AL*, 'Christian marriage, as a reflection of the union between Christ and his Church, is fully realized in the union between a man and a woman who give themselves to each other in a free, faithful and exclusive love, who belong to each other until death and are open to the transmission of life, and are consecrated by the sacrament, which grants them the grace to become a domestic church and a leaven of new life for society' (*AL* 292).[22] According to Francis, this realization constitutes 'the ideal' of marriage.

'The full ideal of marriage' (*AL* 307) should not be confused with an abstract idea, as unrealistic as it might be desirable, which can be admired and pursued in the same way one might pursue utopia which can never be realized. Even the Church has been given to this 'excessive idealization' if it is true, as Francis recognizes, that 'at times we have also proposed a far too abstract and almost artificial theological ideal of marriage, far removed from the concrete situations and practical possibilities of real families' (*AL* 36).

The clue to correctly understanding the full ideal of marriage can be found in the very definition of Christian marriage proposed by *AL* as a 'reflection of the union between Christ and the Church.' This image evokes the passage from the Second Letter to the Corinthians in which Paul illustrates the dynamics proper to Christian life: 'Now the Lord is the Spirit, and where the Spirit of the Lord is, there is freedom. And all of us, with unveiled faces, seeing the glory of the Lord as though reflected in a mirror (*katoptrizómenoi*), are being transformed into the same image (*metamorphoúmetha*) from one degree of

---

22 In this definition, as in previous magisterial documents (cf. LEO XIII, *Arcanum Divinae Sapientiae*, 1880; PIUS XI, *Casti Connubi*, 1930; VATICAN COUNCIL II, *Gaudium et Spes*, 1965; PAUL VI, *Humanae Vitae*, 1968; JOHN PAUL II, *Familiaris Consortio*, 1981), all the fundamental aspects of marriage and family are considered, obviously: the sacramental sign; conjugal union; generation and education of children; social function; ecclesial mission.

glory to another; for this comes from the Lord, the Spirit' (3:17-18). In this illustration, the reflection of the glorious image of Christ in Christians is the gradual – from one degree of glory to another – appearance in them of the transformation wrought by the Spirit of Christ. Given this illustration, Christian marriage reflects the union of Christ with the Church when the Holy Spirit gradually transforms conjugal love according to that image. Its merit is to show how Christian marriage, even when pointed to as an ideal, is understood dynamically, not as a goal not yet reached or which it is far from, but as a process still underway. The ideal of Christian marriage is not the complete achievement of the love given and commanded by Christ, but the continuous conforming of conjugal love to Christ's love. Marriage is an embodied ideal but one not as yet completely so. In fact the ideal of marriage corresponds to conjugal charity whose growth has no limits since charity – according to Aquinas' teaching[23] – is 'a participation in that infinite charity which is the Holy Spirit' (*AL* 134).

COMMITMENT

The dynamic interpretation of the full ideal of marriage is already there in *AL* in the repeated reference to marriage as a 'commitment', and more precisely as 'a stable commitment to share and shape together the whole of life' (*AL* 123). Marriage as a commitment is a projecting towards the spouses' future, projecting themselves forward in shared life. In this sense marriage, more than being a state of life

---

23 THOMAS AQUINAS, *Summa Theologiae*, II-II, 24, 7, c.

could be understood as a movement, a gradual movement of conjugal charity which is incipient, proficient, perfect.[24]

The major emphasis which *AL* assigns to this category of 'commitment' or future projection, compared to the category of 'covenant' introduced by Vatican II, and already innovative by comparison with the earlier category of 'contract',[25] can be interpreted as a further development of the Church's teaching on marriage. If 'covenant' gained us a more personal view of marriage compared to the normative view signified by 'contract', then 'commitment' to a shared future [in Vatican-speak the term used is '*progetto*'] acquires a dynamic view of marriage. Marriage is now more adequately understood as the 'history' of the personal covenant agreed upon by the spouses.

The understanding of marriage as an historical commitment [or 'project'] must not overlook its sacramental background. In fact Christian marriage is a commitment or project fostered by the Holy Spirit who acts especially through the nuptial sacrament. In sacramental marriage the Spirit gives Christ's love, enabling the spouses to love one another as he loves. Christian marriage's commitment to the future, therefore, is not the unfolding of a history of love which a man and a woman decide upon themselves, but their correspondence to Christ's love. In this sense, Christian marriage is not an autonomous 'project' but one of response by the spouses, their way of corresponding to God's plan for their future. There is no subjectivism or relativism in

24 THOMAS AQUINAS, *Summa Theologiae*, II-II, 24, 9.
25 *Codex Iuris Canonici* (1917), can. 1012 § 1.

conceiving of marriage as a gradual process of the couple in conjugal charity, since it is fostered objectively, and guided by the charity of Christ.

Sacrament of faith

The proclamation of Christian marriage as gospel for the family is provided in *AL* by envisaging the sacrament of marriage as gift and vocation. Christian marriage is a gift of divine grace which promotes and sustains the vocation to conjugal love. Reflecting Francis' complex teaching, *AL* draws attention especially to the gratuitousness of the gift and the quality of love it generates. Less attention is given to how divine love is translated into conjugal love. Divine love does not bring about conjugal love without involving the freedom of the spouses, and the freedom of the spouses does not bring about conjugal love without acceptance of divine love. The transfusion of divine love into conjugal love, of Christ's charity into conjugal charity, goes back to Christian faith, and more precisely, in reference to Christian marriage, to the relationship between faith and sacrament.

Already in the past, the importance of the question of faith had been emphasised by the then Prefect of the Congregation for the Doctrine of the Faith, Cardinal Joseph Ratzinger. Reminding us that 'faith belongs to the essence of the sacrament,' he looked forward to 'further studies' to clarify 'whether every marriage between two baptized persons is "ipso facto" a sacramental marriage' and 'what counts as an absence of faith that would hinder a sacramental marriage.'[26]

26 J Ratzinger, «Introduzione», *Sulla pastorale dei divorziati*

Then later, almost as a conclusion to his pontificate, Pope Benedict XVI took up the discussion once again of the relationship between faith (*fides*) and marriage (*foedus*), maintaining that while it is important not to confuse them, 'nevertheless it is not possible to separate them totally.' Far from suggesting 'any facile automatism between the lack of faith and the invalidity of the matrimonial union,' Benedict XVI intended, though, 'to highlight how such a lack may, although not necessarily, also damage the goods of the marriage, since the reference to the natural order desired by God is inherent in the conjugal pact.'[27]

Theological understanding of the relationship between the faith of those preparing for, celebrating and living marriage, and the grace of the sacrament, appears to be decisive regarding the better understanding and more effective proclamation of the gospel of the family.[28] Confirmation

---

risposati. Documenti, commenti e studi, Libreria Editrice Vaticana, Vatican City, 1998, 7-29, 27-28. This part of the introduction is now available on the Holy See's website: 'Concerning some objections to the Church's teaching on the Reception of Holy Communion by Divorced and Remarried Members of the Faithful'.

27 BENEDICT XVI, *Address for the Inauguration of the Judicial Year of the Tribunal of the Roman Rota*, 26 January 2013, nos 1.4.

28 The question of faith is taken up in the work sponsored by the PONTIFICAL COUNCIL FOR THE FAMILY, *Famiglia e Chiesa: un legame indissolubile*. (Family and Church, an indissoluble bond) *Contributo interdisciplinare per l'approfondimento sinodale* (in Famiglia e Vita 7), Libreria Editrice Vaticana, Vatican City, 2015, in particular in two lucid contributions by A BOZZOLO, «Matrimonio: fede, sacramento, disciplina», pp. 27-67; «Matrimonio e sacramento», 491-508, and in interventions (pp. 67-103) and debate (pp. 103-105) by other scholars. As a summary, see A FUMAGALLI, *Il tesoro e la creta. La sfida sul matrimonio dei*

of the importance of this theological development comes from Francis' magisterium, which following *AL* has drawn attention to 'the theme of the relationship between faith and matrimony, especially from the prospective of faith inherent in the human and cultural context, in which the nuptial intention is formed.'[29]

2. *The vitality of love*

True love, corresponding to conjugal charity as experienced in Christian marriage, is part of the eschatological tension in the history of salvation, between the already and the not yet of the coming of the Kingdom. The earthly realization of true love is not, therefore, one of perfection, purity of intention and a consistency proper only to the Kingdom to come, but one of an 'historical journey' which, while keeping alive the striving ... grow[s] and mature[s] in the ability to love' (*AL* 325).

2.1 A gradual process

The gradual process in conjugal charity corresponds to the gradual dynamic of the history of salvation.

GRADUALNESS OF SALVATION IN CHRIST

By going beyond the thesis of the *duplex ordo*, the order of created nature and the order of uplifting grace, contemporary theological anthropology has acquired the biblical and

cristiani (Giornale di Teologia 375), Queriniana, Brescia, 2014, 87-107.

29 FRANCIS, *Address for the Inauguration of the Judicial Year of the Tribunal of the Roman Rota*, 21 January 2017.

patristic thesis of 'creation in Christ'[30] or 'predestination in Christ.'[31] Although unifying, creation/predestination in Christ is not to be confused with the history of salvation, eliminating every distinction. The history of salvation is one, without being uniform. In fact creation in Christ is only the beginning of the history of salvation, but not yet its fulfilment. Already 'in Christ', created nature is not fully 'formed in Christ'.

The unity of the history of salvation in Christ is not provided by short-circuiting the path between its beginning and its fulfilment, but by the dynamic tension which connects the two different poles. The author of this dynamic is the Holy Spirit who configures the history of salvation as a dynamic process. Though not without interruption, it involves different degrees of conformation to and incorporation into Christ. Salvation is not a 'state' one is already placed in, or which one has not been yet elevated to, but it is a 'history' in which the Holy Spirit transforms the rough version into a complete one, leads the incipient incorporation to its fullness, without discontinuity but gradually, by degrees, variously included between the basic one of creation and the completed one of full conformation to Christ. Bearing in mind that salvation in Christ will be complete only with the definitive coming of the Kingdom of heaven, throughout the course of history and until its

30 LF LADARIA, *Antropologia teologica* (Theologica), Piemonte, Casale Monferrato (AI), 1995, 29-47.

31 FG BRAMBILLA, *Antropologia teologica. Chi è l'uomo perché te ne curi?* (Corso di Teologia Sistematica 12), Queriniana, Brescia, 2005, 157-213.

end, incorporation in and conformation to Christ will not be complete.

Human historicity corresponds to the history of salvation in Christ. This has been put in the spotlight, with regard to marriage and the family, in the recent moral teaching of the Church.

LAW OF GRADUALNESS OR A GRADUAL PROCESS

Beginning with the Synod of Bishops on the Christian Family in 1980,[32] and especially in the following Apostolic Exhortation *Familiaris Consortio* (*FC*) by John Paul II in 1981, the historical nature of Christian life, with particular reference to marriage and the family, was indicated in terms of 'gradualness' or step-by-step advance.

From its introduction into the work of the Synod, the category of 'gradualness' has been understood as having two tendencies: one, of a theological and moral kind, referred it to the 'history of the pilgrim people of God'; the other, of a doctrinal and pastoral kind, referred it to the 'doctrine of the Church'.[33] The theological and moral approach considers gradualness to be the historical and salvific dynamic resulting from the actions of human freedom compared to the action of the divine Spirit.[34] The doctrinal and pastoral

---

32 The category 'law of gradualness' appears twice in: SYNOD OF BISHOPS – 5ᵀᴴ ORDINARY GENERAL ASSEMBLY, *List of Propositions* Post disceptationem, Proposition 24, 24 October 1980, in *Enchiridion Vaticanum* 7, nos 747, 749.

33 J RATZINGER, «Il Relazione», *Il Regno – documenti* 25 (1980/21) 488-492, 488-489.

34 J-M LUSTIGER, *Gradualità e conversione*, in *La «Familiaris*

approach considers gradualness to be the pedagogical tool for connecting the insufficient actions of freedom with doctrinal norms.

These two approaches to gradualness and their uncritical juxtaposition are proposed once more in the text of *FC*. Also in John Paul II's Exhortation, gradualness in conversion to the mystery of Christ[35] and gradualness in the fulfilment of the Church's norms[36] do not seem to be brought together adequately. And although one can also discover a certain ambivalence still in *AL* with regard to how gradualness is seen, there is a change of emphasis just the same, in that it prefers to speak of the path of true love, than of doctrinal norms.[37]

The choice of the dynamics of love rather than of static norms gives a different meaning to the 'so-called "law of gradualness."'[38] It does not point to the gradual fulfilment of a norm which is impracticable at the moment but which is later fulfilled. Rather, the law of gradualness refers to gradual growth in love which is always possible but never ultimately complete. Seen this way, the category of a 'gradual process' proposed in *FC* as synonymous with the 'law of gradualness', better explains its meaning.

Conceived of as a gradual process in charity, the law of gradualness does not run the risk of being identified with

Consortio», Libreria editrice Vaticana, Vatican City, 1982, 31-57.

35   Cf. *FC*, no. 9.

36   Cf. *Ibidem*, no. 34.

37   D Bogner, *Un cenno di cambiamento. L'ambivalenza della «gradualità» in Amoris Laetitia*, in S Goertz – C. Witting (eds), *Amoris Laetitia. Un punto di svolta per la teologia morale?*, 163-180.

38   *FC*, no. 34.

what *FC* disapproves of as 'gradualness of the law', 'as if there were different degrees or forms of precept in God's law for different individuals and situations' (no. 34). The divine law, consisting of the gift and the duty to practise the new commandment of love, retains its validity for everyone in whatever situation. But it is not an external norm at some distance from the individual agent, one that must be gradually fulfilled; it is the inner dynamic which fosters the gradual process of the individual agent in love.

This process, certainly a subjective one, is not subjectivistic however, since it corresponds objectively to the love of Christ. For the individual who is making progress, though, the 'objective' is not immediately the entire process but the loving degree that can and must be practised here and now. In other words, there is an 'objective subjectivity'. It does not coincide with absolute objectivity, but nor is it resolved by arbitrary subjectivity and hence moral relativism.

THE PERFECT IMPERFECTION OF CHARITY

Gradual growth in charity is an incomplete process throughout history, because in relation to the perfection which belongs to the definitive coming of the Kingdom of heaven, charity experienced historically is imperfect. Nevertheless, there is a perfection of charity for someone who loves on this side of history. 'Charity is perfect with regard to the person who loves,' Thomas teaches us 'when he loves as much as he can.'[39] The perfection of charity is not the 'perfection of the charity of heaven' but the 'perfection

---

39 THOMAS AQUINAS, *Summa Theologiae*, II-II. 24, 8, c.

of charity that is possible to a wayfarer' in the earthly condition.[40] The perfection of charity in the *homo viator* is realized 'when a man gives his whole heart to God habitually, viz, by neither thinking nor desiring anything contrary to the love of God.'[41] The full ideal of conjugal charity is realized, therefore, when the spouses are constantly ready to love one another as Christ has loved them. This perfection, relative to the measure of freedom, the *habitus* in Scholastic terms, can exist alongside the imperfection involved in carrying it out in the *actus*, that is, with venial sins.[42]

In the dynamic of gradual growth, the perfection of conjugal charity is compatible with the fact that 'no family drops down from heaven perfectly formed; families need constantly to grow and mature in the ability to love' (*AL* 325). Compared to the full ideal of marriage, no situation is perfectly in order and every situation, given its imperfection, can be said to be 'irregular'.[43]

2.2 Discernment in dialogue

Gradual growth in charity can be assessed as perfect when loving action corresponds to the potential of love

40 *Ivi.*
41 *Ivi.*
42 *Ibidem*, II-II, 24, 8, 2, ad 2.
43 'My great joy as a result of this document resides in the fact that it coherently overcomes that artificial, superficial, clear division between "regular" and "irregular", and subjects everyone to the common call of the Gospel, according to the words of St. Paul: "For God has consigned all to disobedience, that He may have mercy on all" (Rom. 11, 32).' C. SCHÖNBORN, Press Conference presenting the post-synodal Apostolic Exhortation *Amoris Laetitia, on love in the family*, 8 April 2016.

made available by the Holy Spirit. The practice of charity in our earthly life is perfect when it corresponds to the grace of the Holy Spirit, in which the new law that urges on and guides the gradual process in love of Christ mainly consists.[44] Understanding of the new law in the concrete existence of individuals is not adequately provided by 'a new set of general rules, canonical in nature and applicable to all cases,' but requires 'a responsible personal and pastoral discernment of particular cases' (*AL* 300). 'To discern means ... listening to the voice of the Spirit and comparing oneself with history and with its demands and challenges, especially those regarding individuals and their concrete life, going beyond abstractions and "cases" ... The hypothesis – and this is very important for the understanding of discernment – is that there is not only a "generic" or universal will of God, but also a special and specific manner in which God's will is impressed on my life with my personality, in my circumstances and my unique vocation.'[45]

THE NEED FOR DISCERNMENT

The gradual progress of charity suggests comparing the practice of discernment with the search for the most adequate stride. The stride should be in accordance with the legs of the person making the journey, meaning it has to be possible, given that, according to the classic utterance

---

44 THOMAS AQUINAS, *Summa Theologiae*, I-II. 106, 1, c.
45 A SPADARO – LJ CAMELI, *La sfida del discernimento in Amoris Laetitia. Esortazione apostolica postsinodale sull'amore nella famiglia. Testo integrale e commento de «La Civiltà Cattolica»* (*Crocevia*), Ancora, Milan, 2106, 242-256, 245-246.

of the Church's moral teaching, *Deus impossibilia non jubet*. The most adequate stride will depend on what the terrain is like, rugged and rough as it may be, and on the physical possibilities of the person making the journey, or, if we put the metaphor aside, it depends on the two reasons which motivate the need for discernment: the particular nature of the case and the degree of responsibility.

The first necessary reason is that discernment makes it possible to remove the uncertainty of the general rule regarding the particular case. Recalling Thomas Aquinas' teaching, Francis reminds us that 'the more we descend to matters of detail, the more frequently we encounter defects' (*AL* 304). Discernment in a particular situation, then, does not detract from the general rule, but is a better recognition of the good to be achieved in the special circumstances of the case which the rule, given its general nature, is unable to consider. In fact the law, as Aquinas once again teaches us, applies in the majority of cases,[46] not in all possible cases. That does not mean that practical discernment arrived at in a particular case can be elevated to the level of a general rule (cf. *AL* 304).

The second necessary reason for particular discernment is given by the fact that 'imputability and responsibility for an action can be diminished or even nullified' (*AL* 302) by mitigating circumstances and conditioning factors. In this regard, the traditional doctrine of the Church teaches that subjective responsibility in corresponding to the objective

---

46   Cf. Thomas Aquinas, *Summa Theologiae*, I-II. 94. 4.

demands of good indicated by the general rule is conditioned by factors which limit awareness and voluntariness.[47] 'A distinction is not always adequately drawn between "voluntary" and "free" acts.' The distinction is immediately clear, instead, if one considers that 'A person may clearly and willingly desire something evil, but do so as the result of an irresistible passion or a poor upbringing. In such cases, while the decision is voluntary, inasmuch as it does not run counter to the inclination of their desire, it is not free, since it is practically impossible for them not to choose that evil … Their decision is voluntary but not free' (*AL* 273).

Discernment of the new law, justified by the particular nature of the situation and personal responsibility, stands apart both from situational ethics and from ethical individualism. For situational ethics, the lack of adequacy of the general rule justifies attributing the individual with the faculty of establishing his or her own rule for dealing with the particular situation in which they find themselves. More radically still. Ethical individualism rejects every general rule, choosing precisely the individual as the unquestionable legislator of his or her actions.

THE PECULIAR NATURE OF DISCERNMENT

Discernment, as envisaged by *AL*, is doubly described as personal and pastoral. This twofold description of discernment goes back to the distinction and peculiar nature of the subjective activities implied.

---

47   Cf. *CCC*, nos 1735; 2352.

Personal discernment is of the kind exercised in the conscience of the moral individual who, as a faithful Christian, seeks God's will in the particular situation in which he or she finds him or herself.[48] Pastoral discernment is carried out by ecclesial agents, bishops and priests in particular, who express the Church's teaching and guidelines from bishops in particular situations experienced by the faithful.

The distinction made between personal and pastoral discernment should not be understood as the simple juxtaposition of two different subjective activities, one by the faithful the other by their pastors. The distinction is rather to be understood literally in terms of a dialogue, a discussion between partners, although they play an asymmetric role in that dialogue. Pastoral discernment serves personal discernment. This latter, without being individualistic, is the place where a practical synthesis occurs between God's will listened to in conscience, and proclaimed by the Church.

Discernment, which is both personal and pastoral, has its place in the 'conversation' between priest and faithful 'in the internal forum' (*AL* 300).[49] The dialogical nature of discernment allows the latter to 'better understand their situation and discover a path to personal growth' and the former to 'understand their plight and their point of view,

---

48 B PETRA, *Amoris Laetitia: accompagnare, discernere e integrare la fragilità* (Cantiere Coppia), Cittadella, Assisi (PG), 2016, 10-11.

49 K NYKIEL, *Foro interno*, in PENITENZIERIA APOSTOLICA (ed.), *Peccato Misericordia Riconciliazione. Dizionario teologico-pastorale*, Libreria Editrice Vaticana, Vatican City, 2016, 185-189,

in order to help them live better lives and to recognize their proper place in the Church' (*AL* 312).

In the conversation in the internal forum, it is up to priests to 'accompany [the individuals concerned] in helping them to understand their situation according to the teaching of the Church and the guidelines of the bishop,' and it is up to the faithful to make 'an examination of conscience through moments of reflection and repentance.'

Proper discernment demands of both priest and faithful, 'fundamental attitudes' of 'humility, discretion and love for the Church and her teaching in a sincere search for God's will and a desire to make a more perfect response to it.' Without these necessary guarantees, discernment succumbs to the 'grave danger' of pastoral individualism on the part of the priest, and personal subjectivism on the part of the faithful, giving rise to the idea that 'the Church maintains a double standard' (*AL* 300), one publicly declared and the other privately practised.

The aim of discernment

Personal and pastoral discernment have the possible good as their aim. The possible good is not the absolute good, that is, good defined quite apart from the individual who puts it into practice; it corresponds rather to the moral dynamic proper to the human person, who does not immediately carry out all that is good but advances gradually in doing so. The possible good, no matter how minimal by comparison

---

185. For the specific reference to *AL* see: B Petra, *Amoris laetitia: accompagnare, discernere e integrare la fragilità*, 11-17.

with the absolute good, is nevertheless the greatest good possible for the individuals doing it. Therefore, although little by comparison with the absolute good, the possible good can be described as the best good.

Within the gradual process of Christian life, the possible good, as has already been suggested, can be compared to the stride chosen by the wayfarer according to his or her possibilities. When seen in terms of the entire journey that has to be taken, the stride adopted is minimal and insufficient. But seen in terms of the stride the individual is capable of, it is more than sufficient, and is in fact the most adequate possible.

The possible good can be further defined, bearing in mind that – according to *AL* – discernment aims at 'the formation of a correct judgment on what hinders the possibility of a fuller participation in the life of the Church and on what steps can foster it and make it grow' (*AL* 300). Discernment, then, has a double aim: negatively speaking it shows that 'a given situation does not correspond objectively to the overall demands of the Gospel'; positively speaking, it recognises 'with sincerity and honesty what for now is the most generous response which can be given to God, and come to see with a certain moral security that it is what God himself is asking amid the concrete complexity of one's limits, while yet not fully the objective ideal' (*AL* 303).

Discernment of particular cases, avoiding thinking 'that everything is black and white', preferring to identify 'elements that can foster evangelization and human and spiritual growth' (*AL* 293), helps 'find possible ways of responding to God and growing in the midst of limits.' For the benefit of such seeking, it needs to be remembered that 'a small step, in the midst of great human limitations, can be more pleasing to God than a life which appears outwardly in order, but moves through the day without confronting great difficulties' (*AL* 305).

Discernment does not stop at identifying a single step, but continues on to indicate steps to follow. Hence, 'discernment is dynamic; it must remain ever open to new stages of growth and to new decisions which can enable the ideal to be more fully realized' (*AL* 303). Moral discernment avoids the binary logic of 'absolutely yes or absolutely no,' corresponding instead to the logic of the *magis*, the 'more', which leads to choosing what is best.

2.3 Personal conscience

In the gradual path of charity, discernment of what is best is not resolved by applying a general rule to the particular case, since it requires correspondence to the potential of love made available by the Holy Spirit and that is possible for personal freedom. The rule certainly encourages the recognition and practice of charity which the Holy Spirit leads someone to perform, but it does not replace his impulse and voice. That is also true for the precepts of the natural law which – Francis maintains, quoting a recent document of the International Theological Commission[50] – cannot 'be presented as an already established set of rules that impose themselves *a priori* on the moral subject; rather, it is a source

---

50 INTERNATIONAL THEOLOGICAL COMMISSION, "In search

of objective inspiration for the deeply personal process of making decisions' (*AL* 305).

ASCRIBING VALUE TO CONSCIENCE

Adequate attention to the voice of the Spirit necessarily goes back to seeing the value of the individual conscience, which *AL* hopes will be adequately formed and involved.[51] Encouraging the Church's pastoral magisterium to take 'a healthy dose of self-criticism' (*AL* 36), Francis laments how it struggles 'to make room for the consciences of the faithful, who very often respond as best they can to the Gospel amid their limitations, and are capable of carrying out their own discernment in complex situations.' As a remedy for this reluctance, Francis maintains that 'individual conscience needs to be better incorporated into the Church's praxis' including 'certain situations which do not objectively embody our understanding of marriage' (*AL* 303).

In today's culture, inclined to individualism (cf. *AL* 33), one could understand this appeal for a better involvement of the individual conscience as attributing to individuals the

of a Universal Ethic: a New Look at the Natural Law", http://www.vatican.va/roman_curia/congregations/cfaith/cti_documents/rc_con_cfaith_doc_20090520_legge-naturale_en.html

51 A Autiero, *Amoris laetitia e la coscienza etica. Una questione di prospettiva*, in S Goertz – C Witting (eds), *Amoris Laetitia. Un punto di svolta per la teologia morale?*, 80-94; F Occhetta, *La coscienza morale e l'amore umano*, in *Amoris laetitia. Esortazione apostolica postsinodale sull'amore nella famiglia. Testo integrale e commento de «La Civiltà Cattolica»* (Crocevia), Ancora, Milan, 2016, 303-313; A Thomasset, *La coscienza morale et les questions posées par les documents récents du magistère romain*, in *Revue d'ethique et de théologie morale* (2017/1) 25-42.

faculty of deciding, in a fully autonomous way, on what good must be done. Francis' teaching does not head in this direction. He speaks of 'involvement', not 'arbitrariness' where the individual conscience is concerned, already suggesting the notion of a 'relational' rather than an 'autonomous' conscience. Obviously in tune with the Church's doctrine, Francis encourages 'the development of an enlightened conscience, formed and guided by the responsible and serious discernment of one's pastor,' encouraging 'an ever greater trust in God's grace' (*AL* 303). If, on the one hand, the claim of 'replacing' consciences is averted, on the other, there is an invitation to 'form' consciences (cf. *AL* 37). The need for formation of individual conscience corresponds to its nature, and it is appropriate now to draw attention to this.

The relational nature of conscience

In referring to conscience, Francis recalls the famous definition of the Second Vatican Council,[52] according to which conscience is 'the most secret core and sanctuary of a person. There each one is alone with God, whose voice echoes in the depths of the heart' (*AL* 222).

The metaphor of the sanctuary, although it points to the most profound and secret inner nature of the human being, does not present it as a private cell, deprived of other presences. On the contrary, it is inhabited by none other than the presence of God. Augustine, the first great Christian theologian to explore the mystery of conscience, speaks of the conscience as '*intimior intimo meo et superior summo*

---

52 Cf. *GS*, no. 16.

meo',[53] linking human intimacy with divine transcendence. The Church's theological and magisterial tradition, though with differing emphases, invites us to conceive of conscience in dialogical terms, as a discourse between God and the human being.

The dialogical nature of conscience can be further explained by considering the other metaphor, a very classical one, which is the metaphor of the voice. With regard to God's voice it does not say that it 'sounds', but that it resounds or 'echoes', letting us understand how God does not speak directly in the intimacy of the human being, but utters a mystical oracle or inner locution. God's voice corresponds better to an echo which is not caused by a simple sound, but by the rebounding of a sound on which one reflects: conscience can be understood as the 'echo of the Spirit.'[54] In fact the Spirit, by reaching out to the human being involved in action, encounters that being's freedom, 'rebounding' or 'resounding' differently according to how the human being acts in the light of this echo. In the case of human actions corresponding to the good urged by the Spirit, there will be a good conscience which quietens the individual, leaving him or her in joy and peace. In the case of actions which go against the good being urged by the Spirit, there will be a bad conscience, which leaves the person restless, causing sorrow and uneasiness, typically known as remorse.

---

53   AUGUSTINE, *Confessions*, 3, 6.
54   A FUMAGALLI, *L'eco dello Spirito. Teologia della coscienza morale* (Biblioteca di Teologia Contemporanea 158), Queriniana, Brescia, 2012.

Conscience testifies to the urgings of the Spirit, and is effectively the echo of these when the conscience is formed. Its adequate formation is aided by acceptance of the Holy Spirit and corresponding to him, or in other words, by listening to the Word, especially in sacramental worship, through relationships in the Christian community, and especially with the Magisterium. The indispensable teaching of the Magisterium, which presents and guarantees moral norms in the Church, instructs the conscience so that it can better judge the good to be done in particular cases in personal existence.[55]

3. *The vulnerability of love*

Although by comparison with the full ideal of marriage, every situation is in some way 'irregular', Canon Law reserves such a description for matrimonial situations of the baptized who are living together *more uxorio* without the sacrament of marriage, therefore not corresponding as yet (as in the case of simple cohabitation and civil marriage), or no longer corresponding (as in the case of a new union of someone who had been sacramentally married) to the Church's teaching. The specific vulnerability of these situations is due to them not enjoying the grace which is proper to the sacrament of marriage.

---

[55] M Chiodi, «Coscienza e norma. Quale rapporto? A proposito del cap. VIII di "Amoris laetitia"», *La Rivista del Clero Italiano* 98/5 (2017) 325-338.

3.1 A range of vulnerabilities

Given the countless variety and practical circumstances of these situations, some 'radically contradict' the ideal of Christian marriage, while others 'realize it in at least a partial and analogous way' (*AL* 292). By recognizing that God's mercy reaches out to everyone and that no one is excluded, the Church tackles such marriage situations through a 'constructive response,' appreciating 'those signs of love which in some way reflect God's own love,' seeking to transform them into 'opportunities that can lead to the full reality of marriage and family in conformity with the Gospel.'

Discernment regarding those simply living together and those who have contracted civil marriage needs to consider that their choice 'is often not motivated by prejudice or resistance to a sacramental union, but by cultural or contingent situations' (*AL* 294). In any case, 'when such unions attain a particular stability, legally recognized, are characterized by deep affection and responsibility for their offspring, and demonstrate an ability to overcome trials, they can provide occasions for pastoral care with a view to the eventual celebration of the sacrament of marriage' (*AL* 293).

What is possible for those simply living together and others who have contracted civil marriage is not possible for the faithful who have divorced and entered a new union, given the impossibility of dissolving their previous sacramental marriage if it is canonically valid.[56] Discernment of the

---

56 "A marriage that is *ratum et consummatum* can be

steps to take in this case represents the most delicate and controversial point of the Exhortation. Already, Benedict XVI's clear teaching had recognized that there are no 'easy recipes'.[57]

In the clear awareness that the new union of divorcees 'is not the ideal which the Gospel proposes for marriage and the family,' discernment must be carried out 'by adequately distinguishing' the 'variety of situations' in such a way that they are not 'pigeonholed or fit into overly rigid classifications.' One has to recognize, for example, that 'one thing is a second union consolidated over time, with new children, proven fidelity, generous self-giving, Christian commitment, a consciousness of its irregularity and of the great difficulty of going back without feeling in conscience that one would fall into new sins … Another thing is a new union arising from a recent divorce, with all the suffering and confusion which this entails for children and entire families, or the case of someone who has consistently failed in his obligations to the family' (*AL* 298).

3.2 The logic of integration

Accepting the direction taken by the majority of the Fathers at the Synod, Pope Francis clearly envisages,

---

dissolved by no human power and by no cause, except death" (Code of Canonn Law, can. 1141). Cf. JOHN PAUL II, *Address to the Tribunal of the Roman Rota for the opening of the Judicial Year*, 21 January, 2000.

57 BENEDICT XVI, *Address to the 7th World Meeting of Families*, Milan (2 June 20112), response 5, in *Insegnamenti* VIII (2012/1), 691. Can be found on the Holy See's website.

including for divorced faithful in a new union, 'the logic of integration' as 'the key to their pastoral care' (*AL* 299). By promoting progress along the *via caritatis*, 'pastoral discernment filled with merciful love' (*AL* 312), he avoids the logic of marginalization and instead pursues the logic of merciful integration within the life of the Church (cf. *AL* 296), which, furthermore, is true for 'everyone, in whatever situation they find themselves' (*AL* 297). Supported by mercy, 'the Church is not a tollhouse' where 'we act as arbiters of grace rather than its facilitators', but 'it is the house of the Father, where there is a place for everyone, with all their problems' (*AL* 310). Even for someone who 'flaunts an objective sin' there is the possibility, encouraged by pastoral discernment, of identifying 'some way of taking part in the life of the community' (*AL* 297).

The logic of integration with regard to divorced faithful in a new union is not a novelty of *AL*, given that it was already clearly at work in the Apostolic Exhortation *FC*. John Paul II wrote there, that 'together with the Synod, I earnestly call upon pastors and the whole community of the faithful to help the divorced, and with solicitous care to make sure that they do not consider themselves as separated from the Church, for as baptized persons they can, and indeed must, share in her life' (no. 84). The authoritative teaching of *FC*, while fostering the integration of divorced and remarried faithful within the life of the Church, poses limits to their admission to the sacraments and taking up roles in the Church.[58]

58 Divorced and remarried faithful were not admitted to

With regard to the discipline of *FC*, already the recent lengthy (two sessions) Synod of Bishops had considered that there was a need 'to discern which of the various forms of exclusion, currently practised in the liturgical, pastoral, educational and institutional framework, can be surpassed.'[59]

Francis accepted this request of the Synod, explaining in two points in *AL* that discernment on involvement of divorced and remarried faithful in the life of the Church can also involve access to the sacraments.

The first point is when the Pope, picking up on the statement by the Synod Fathers that 'the degree of responsibility is not equal in all cases' observes that 'the consequences or effects of a rule need not necessarily always be the same' (*AL* 300). Explaining this criterion in a note, Pope Francis says that 'This is also the case with regard to sacramental discipline, since discernment can recognize that in a particular situation no grave fault exists' (*AL* 300, note 336).

---

the sacraments, not only to a new sacrament of marriage, but also reception of other sacraments, especially the sacrament of Eucharist and Reconciliation. Admission to Eucharistic Communion and to sacramental Confession, to be truthful, was not absolutely excluded, but tied to two conditions: abstinence from acts proper to spouses and avoiding creating an obstacle – 'scandal' in the language of Canon Law – for other faithful. The discipline established by *FC* also requires that divorced and remarried individuals not take on roles in the Church in areas requiring a particular witness of Christian life: the liturgical area (reader, extraordinary Eucharistic minister); the pastoral area (member of pastoral councils); the educational area (catechist, godparents for sacraments of Christian initiation); the institutional area (religion teacher).

[59] SYNOD OF BISHOPS - 14TH ORDINARY GENERAL ASSEMBLY, *The Vocation and Mission of the Family in the Church and the Contemporary World*, Final report, no. 84

The second point is when the Pope reflects on the possibility that 'because of forms of conditioning and mitigating factors,' it is possible for someone not to be (fully) guilty of 'the objective situation of sin' in which they find themselves and can, therefore, 'be living in God's grace, can love and ... also grow in the life of grace and charity, while receiving the Church's help to this end' (*AL* 305). Explaining the nature of this help. Francis states that 'in certain cases, this can include the help of the sacraments' (*AL* 305, note 351).[60]

The logic of discernment, also regarding the sacraments for divorced and remarried faithful, does not correspond to the generic question of 'whether one can or cannot', but measures pastoral discipline by the degree of maturity of personal responsibility along the gradual journey of love. Therefore, the possible admission of divorced and remarried faithful to areas of Christian life thus far excluded, and especially to the sacramental area, is not a new canonical regulation established by Francis, but the result of a journey, the fruit of personal and pastoral discernment.

---

60 In both points in which the integration of divorced and remarried faithful concerns the sacraments, Francis quotes two paragraphs from *EG*, nos 44 and 47, regarding the sacrament of Reconciliation and the sacrament of the Eucharist respectively. In no. 44 the Pope reminds priests that the confessional must not be a torture chamber, but rather an encounter with the Lord's mercy'; in no. 47, he likewise remarks that the Eucharist 'is not a prize for the perfect, but a powerful medicine and nourishment for the weak.'

3.3 Shared responsibility

This indication of the demanding way of particular discernment instead of general rules is not an abdication on Francis' part of his magisterial authority, but involvement in the Church's journey of responsibility on the part of everyone:[61] the faithful involved, who must question their conscience regarding their marriage situation; pastoral workers who accompany them on their journey of personal maturity; priests who carry out the discernment; bishops who have the task of offering guidelines which integrate the Pope's teaching for the benefit of local Churches.

The pastoral magisterium of *AL* already contains essential indications for the practice of discernment, which it nevertheless seems appropriate to integrate so that, especially in the various local Churches, there can be avoidance of an excessive lack of pastoral homogeneity, encouraging instead a greater ecclesial communion. That would not only comfort priests in carrying out pastoral discernment, but would encourage the awareness of a journey in the faithful involved and in Christian communities. It might be a very personal journey, but it is not an individual one. It is an ecclesial journey.

---

61 HJ POTTMEYER, «Popolo di Dio in cammino. La comprensione della Chiesa di papa Francesco come chiave di lettura di *Amoris laetitia*» in S GOERTZ – C WITTING (eds), *Amoris Laetitia. Un punto di svolta per la teologia morale?*, cit. 249-256. On the notion of the Church implied in the Exhortation, also: V PAGLIA – M YAÑEZ – L BRESSAN – P SEQUERI, *Il legame famigliare del popolo di Dio. Prospettive ecclesiologiche nell'Amoris Laetitia* (Famiglia e Vita), Libreria Editrice Vaticana, Vatican City, 2016.

It seems appropriate, then, to also refer what *AL* explicitly establishes for the preparation of engaged couples for marriage and for procedures for null and void marriages, to the pastoral care of the divorced and remarried faithful. It assigns to each local Church the task of improving discernment of the best way, amongst all the possible ways, of doing these things (cf. *AL* 207). The involvement of local Churches corresponds, furthermore, to the notion of the universal Church as a 'polyhedron'. It is not a monolithic uniformity but a multicultural people, whose common journey cannot be constrained within a single way of doing things and all following the same rhythm, but needs to be accompanied by 'each country or region' seeking 'solutions better suited to its culture and sensitive to its traditions and local needs' (*AL* 3).

CHAPTER 3
CONCLUDING SUMMARY

The Gospel, the glorious proclamation of God's love for humankind, is the *raison d'etre* and essential mission of the Church in the world. Inviting the whole Church to 'a new chapter of evangelization', in *Evangelii Gaudium* (*EG*, 1), Francis also asks theology to be a genuine 'evangelizing theology', a theology 'from the Gospel' and 'of the Gospel', evangelically generated and shaped. The theology promoted by Francis is already there like a watermark in his magisterium, welling up from 'the heart of the Gospel (*EG* 34-39). It is a 'radical theology' closer to its radical Gospel roots than it is to its doctrinal ramifications.

At its roots, Francis' theology does not replace 'scholarly efforts to advance dialogue with the world of cultures and sciences' (*EG* 133). Francis is referring to the more critical elaboration of theology according to which the image of the Church is 'the body of Christ' in which it is given to 'its members' (1 Cor 27-28) 'that some would be apostles, some prophets, some evangelists, some pastors and teachers' (Eph 4:11).

Francis' magisterium, while recognizing and promoting theology, reminds it of its essential roots, so that its various branches do not end up hiding and smothering it. This reminder of its roots at the same time avoids theology developing apart from them as an ideal system and abstract theory.

The distinction which Francis reminds us of between the roots and the branches, between the proclamation of the gospel and its critical reasoning, highlights the possibility of and opportunity for theological pluralism which, to those who long for a 'monolithic body of doctrine' could seem 'undesirable and leading to confusion' but in reality 'serves to bring out and develop different facets of the inexhaustible riches of the Gospel' (*EG* 40). On the other hand, theological ramifications, insofar as they develop their gospel roots, suffer the limitation of any of the Church's teachings, that they are not 'easily understood or readily appreciated by everyone,' regardless of the assent of faith to the gospel, 'beyond the range of clear reasons and arguments.' This is further reason for more developed theological doctrine to nurture 'the teacher's way of life' which aims at reawakening 'the assent of the heart by its nearness, love and witness' (*EG* 42).

Francis' radical theology, by focusing on the joyful proclamation of 'the God of love who saves us', is specified in a moral theology that interprets, weighs up and communicates Christian activity, its proper object, as a 'response of love' (*EG* 39).

1. *The interpretation of Christian morality*

The interpretation of Christian morality as a response of love invites us to consider its twofold nature, response and love: it is about 'response' and a 'response of love'.

The interpretation of human activity as a 'response' of love gives primacy to God's love: 'The activity of the Christian is first of all a secondary act of response to the primary action of God in man.'[1] It follows from this that 'The life of the Church should always reveal clearly that God takes the initiative, that "he has loved us first" (1 Jn 4:19) and that he alone "gives the growth" (1 Cor 3:7)' (*EG* 12).

Recognition of the Holy Spirit as the basis of Christian morality corresponds to the primacy of God's love in the interpretation of human activity. It is up to the Spirit, in fact, to bring about the living presence of Christ which pours out God's love, in history, in every time and place. The Holy Spirit's gift of love communicates to human beings the grace of responding to love, incorporating them into Christ and conforming them to him in the way they love. The primacy of God's love in interpreting human activity re-awakens moral theology to pay attention to the grace of the Holy Spirit.

The spiritual inspiration for the moral theology which Francis points to and asks for, stands out for its reference to the past and the future of the Church's moral tradition. In reference to the past, Francis recovers for moral theology the 'new law' which consists principally of the 'grace of the Holy Spirit'. Posited by Thomas Aquinas as the key to the moral law, it had been subsequently lost sight of. In reference to the future, Francis promotes the post-conciliar development of moral theology, according to the indication given by Paul VI, for which 'the christology and especially the ecclesiology of the Council must be followed by a new study and new cult of the Holy Spirit as the inevitable complement to Council

---

1 HU von Balthasar, *Only Love is Credible*, Ignatius Press, 2014, 113.

teaching.'[2] Continuing along these lines, John Paul II, in the first encyclical in the Church's history dedicated entirely to 'fundamental questions of the Church's moral teaching', established among 'essential elements of Revelation in the Old and New Testament with regard to moral action ... the gift of the Holy Spirit, source and means of the moral life of the "new creation" (cf. 2 Cor 5:17).'[3]

The primacy of God's love shapes human action not simply as a response, but as a response of love. What qualifies Christian activity, as its radiating centre, is the love of Christ which, when accepted in faith, becomes love among Christians. In Christian life, love enjoys primacy, and is at the top of the 'hierarchy' of truths which according to Francis applies to both the dogmas of faith and the Church's moral teaching (cf. *EG* 36). Referring to the authoritative lesson of Thomas Aquinas,[4] Pope Bergoglio teaches that 'the Church's moral teaching has its own "hierarchy", in the virtues and in the acts which proceed from them' (*EG* 37).

The virtuous love of Christians, at the top of the hierarchy of moral truths, can be more specifically indicated as virtues of charity and mercy. The virtue of charity, inasmuch as it is the virtue which unites us with God, is 'the most excellent of the virtues.'[5] It 'extends to all works of virtue,'[6] to the point

---

2   PAUL VI, General Audience, 6 June 1973; cf. also *Marialis Cultus*, 22 March 1974, nos. 26, 27; JOHN PAUL II, *Dominum et Vivificantem*, 18 May 1986, no. 2.

3   JOHN PAUL II, *Veritatis Splendor* (*VS*), no. 28.

4   THOMAS AQUINAS, *Summa Theologiae*, I-II, 66, 4-6.

5   *Ibidem*, II-II, 23, 6, c.

6   *Ibidem*, II-II, 23, 4, 2.

where 'no true virtue is possible without charity'[7]: *'caritas forma virtutum.'*[8] Charity, as love of God given to human beings and involving them in love of their neighbour, shines out specially in the virtue of mercy. 'Of all the virtues which relate to our neighbour, mercy is the greatest.' In fact by coming to the aid of others in their misery, mercy reveals charity in all its potential. It is no coincidence that 'mercy is accounted as being proper to God: and therein His omnipotence is declared to be chiefly manifested.'[9] In the light of what has been observed, the primacy of love in the interpretation of Christian morality can be determined by saying that if charity unites us to God it is superior to mercy shown to our neighbour, inasmuch as charity shown to the wretched can be considered 'as the sum total of the Christian religion.'[10]

As is the case with growth in charity, its translation into mercy too is a dramatic and dynamic process, a story of love promoted by the grace of the Holy Spirit and met by human freedom. The interpretation of Christian morality as a story of love gains for moral theology a dynamic notion of Christian life not fragmented into individual acts but made up of a gradual process. The same interpretation, far from seeing Christian morality as the observance of an impersonal law, conceives of it rather as a personal loving relationship of the Christian with God and with neighbour.

7   *Ibidem*, II-II, 23, 7, c.
8   *Ibidem*, II-II, 23, 8.
9   *Ibidem*, II-II, 30, 4, c.
10 *Ibidem*, II-II, 30, 4, ad 2.

2. Appraisal of moral action

Moral theology, beyond its being an interpretative science, is a science of appraisal. It not only studies the foundation and structures of moral activity in the light of Christian Revelation but comes to a judgement on moral activity in the light of the same.

The essential view of Christian morality as a response of love shapes appraisal by moral theology as a judgement on the loving correspondence of the human being to God's merciful love. The human response of love cannot be judged by limiting it only to the outward nature of actions, but must also include the inner disposition which these outward actions reveal. Moral action cannot be reduced to the actions that have been carried out, but looks at the intentions inscribed in them. Love, which is also manifested through these actions, has its roots in the heart.

Given its deeply personal roots, the human response of love to God's love cannot be judged by a set of rules which lies outside individuals, but through an inner judgement of the individuals themselves, something the moral doctrine of the Church attributes to conscience. Judgement on moral activity cannot be carried out by a third person but must be arrived at in the first person.

It is up to the individual conscience, the echo of the Holy Spirit in the intimacy of the human being, to arrive at a judgement on the correspondence of actions to the love of Christ given and commanded by the Holy Spirit. The judgement of conscience looks at individual actions. In traditional terms of the Church's moral teaching, it is 'the ultimate concrete judgement'[11] which best approximates the single action. Inasmuch as it is 'ultimate' and 'concrete', the judgement of conscience contemplates a prior process of judgement instructed by the divine law, and made known to human beings through the precepts of the natural law and the commandments of the law revealed in the Old and New Testaments, which the Church, guaranteed by its Magisterium, authoritatively teaches.

Law and conscience are not two rival authorities, the former divine, the latter human, but two expressions of the one authority of the Spirit, the former more general and the latter more focused. Again in terms of the Church's traditional moral teaching, this distinction and correlation can be found in the definition of the law and conscience as a 'universal norm' and 'proximate norm'[12] respectively, of moral action.

In the magisterial teaching of the Church proposed by Francis, recognising individual conscience as the last word is not a misunderstanding of the words of the law. Conscience sees in the concreteness of action what the law teaches it to see. Far from being in competition, law and conscience work together for the same end, that of helping the person to know the best response that can and must be given to God's love in the concreteness of acting.

The primacy of conscience in the judgement made about individual actions does not therefore do away with 'the existence of objective moral norms which are valid for

11 *VS*, no. 63.
12 *Ibidem*, no. 60

everyone' (*EG* 64). Rather does it attest to the fact that the judgement on love practised or otherwise by the individual in response to God's love, is not adequately achieved unless instruction by the general norms of the law is integrated into the particular discernment of conscience. The law, which comes first in instructing moral judgement, comes second to the judgement of conscience.

3. Communicating moral theology

The interpretation and appraisal of Christian morality as a 'response of love' also informs the communicative style of moral theology. If the response of love is the essential truth of Christian morality, then moral theological discourse should focus on it, all the more so when in dialogue with our contemporary media culture, whose speed and selection of content tends to distort the Church's moral teaching, reducing it to 'some of its secondary aspects' (*EG* 34).

So that the essential truth of Christian morality is not blurred, the Church's constant discernment is needed, to review 'certain customs not directly connected to the heart of the Gospel' and prune rules or precepts 'which may have been quite effective in their time, but no longer have the same usefulness for directing and shaping people's lives' (*EG* 43). The hierarchy of truths requires that in proclaiming the Gospel, which moral theology too is aiming at, 'a fitting sense of proportion' has to be given the essential truth, recognizable 'in the frequency with which certain themes are brought up and in the emphasis given to them in preaching' (*EG* 38).

The quintessence of Christian morality is condensed in the new commandment of Jesus: 'that you love one another as I have loved you' (Jn 15:12). This 'first' and 'greatest' commandment which best identifies Christians as such, – 'By this everyone will know that you are my disciples, if you have love for one another' (Jn 13:35) – is the reason why 'whenever the New Testament authors want to present the heart of the Christian moral message, they present the essential requirement of love for one's neighbour' (*EG* 161).[13]

Focused essentially on Christian love, the most adequate and effective communication of the moral message of the Gospel is characterized by a 'positive language', not so much aimed at what 'shouldn't be done' but rather at 'what we can do better,' and such that even when it indicates a prohibition restraining us from evil, it also points to a positive and attractive value (cf. *EG* 159).

The original theological style of Pope Francis can raise questions about the continuity or otherwise of his magisterium compared to preceding magisterial tradition. That is true above all for his moral magisterium, especially in the area of the family and marriage, notoriously one of the most delicate and debated areas within and beyond the Church. The interpretations of Francis' moral magisterium do not seem to hit the mark, neither in the case where continuity without innovation is discovered compared with earlier magisterial tradition, nor in the case where a discontinuous novelty is seen. The theological thinking that shines through Francis' moral magisterium could be better

---

13 Cf, Rom 13:8, 10; Jas 2:8; Gal 5:14; 1 Thess 3:12.

compared to a hairpin bend on a mountain road. While the road continues, there is a sharp turning point from which we gain a new perspective and panorama. Taking advantage of all the previous Tradition, Francis' moral teaching extends the gradual journey of the Church in keeping with the promise of Christ to draw all people to himself from the height of his love (cf. Jn 12:32).

www.ingramcontent.com/pod-product-compliance
Lightning Source LLC
Chambersburg PA
CBHW052028290426
44112CB00014B/2420